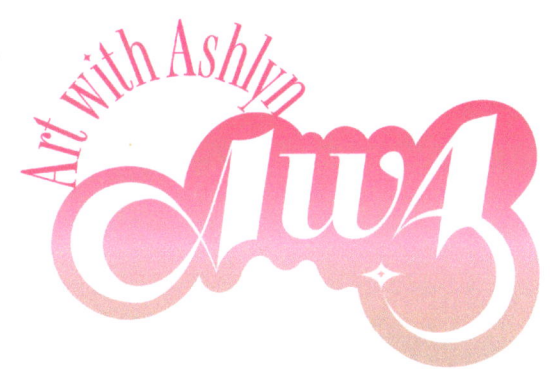

Illustration & Design
Brand Identity, Surface Design, & Advertising
AwA Portfolio 2024 *

*Trigger Warning: Written poems may reference explicit Sexual Assault, Suicide, & Violence.

@art.with.ashlyn   www.artwithashlyn.com   artwithashlyn.co@gmail.com

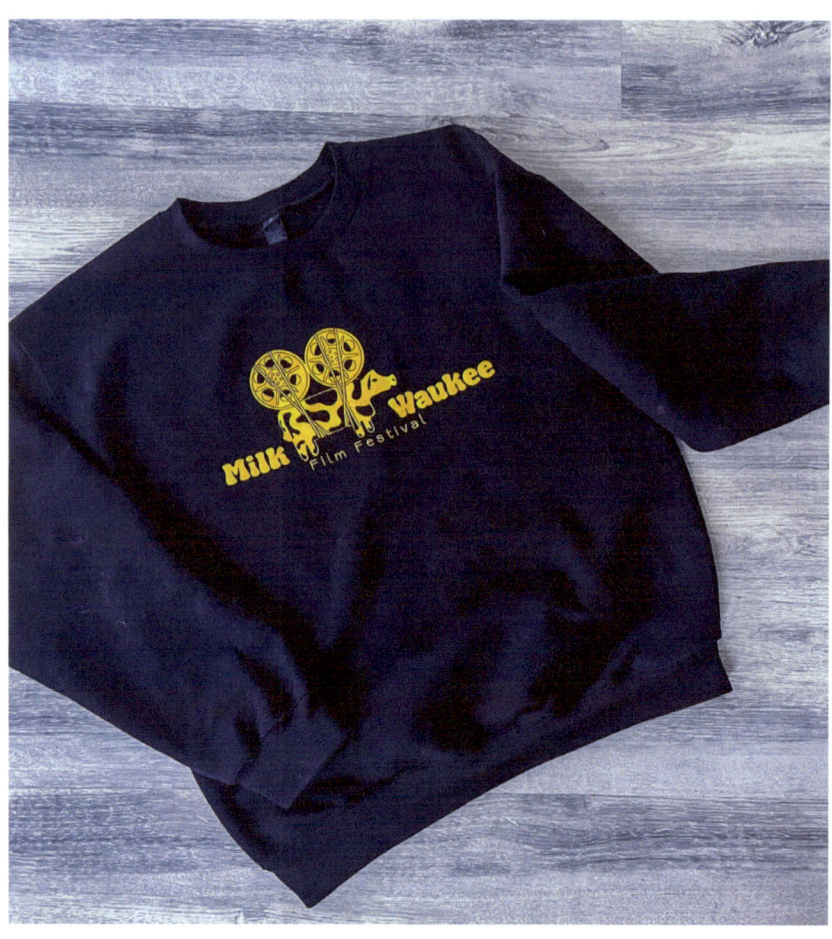
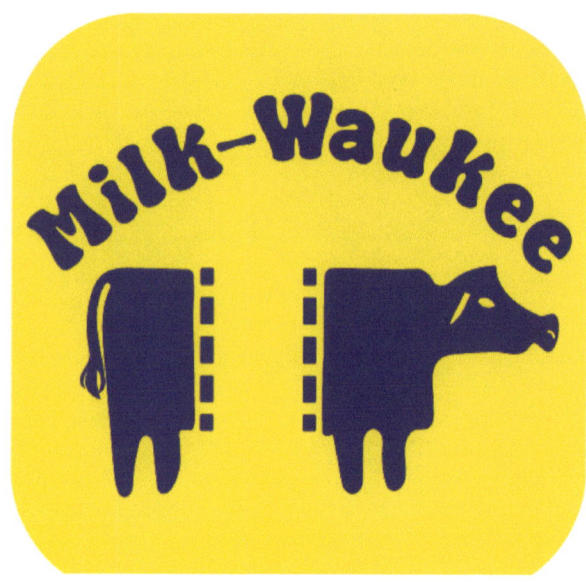
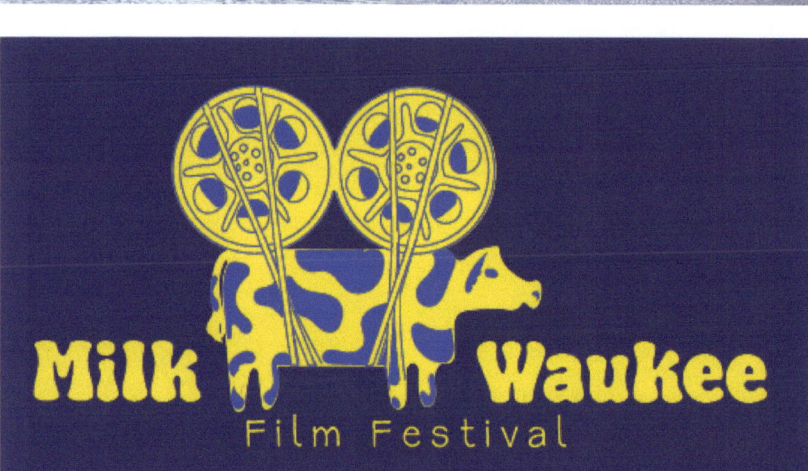
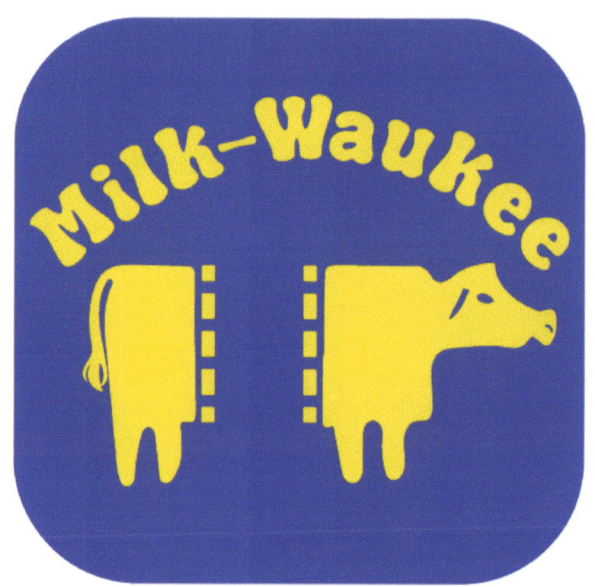
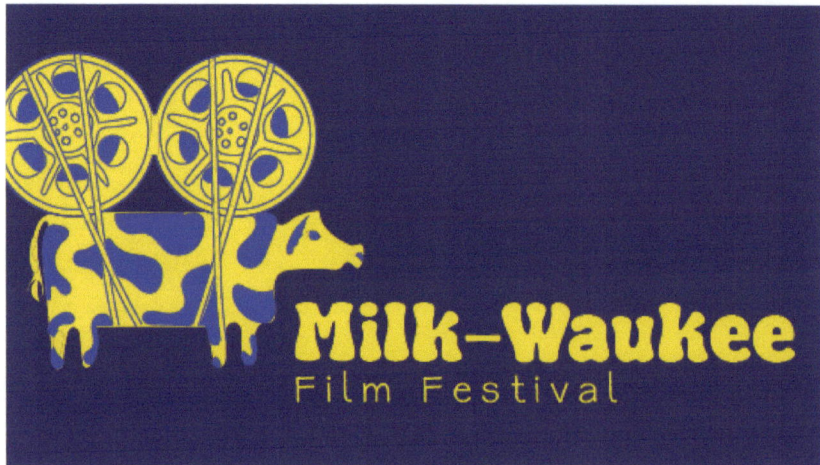
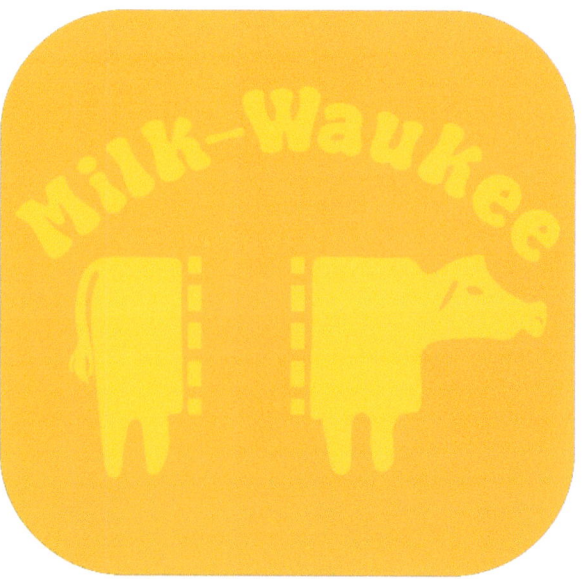

UWM Milk-Waukee Film Festival Brand Identity. Adobe Illustrator.

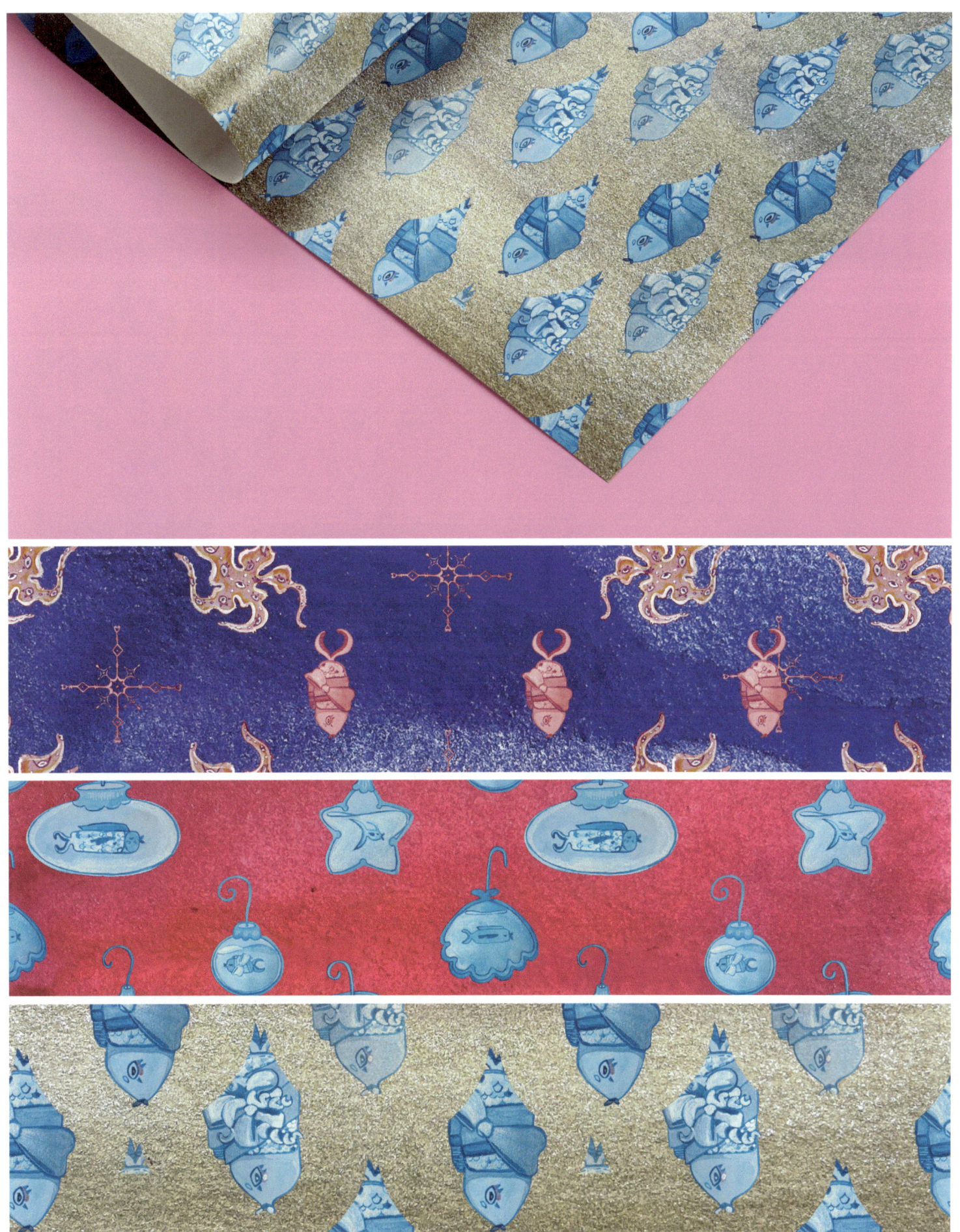

"Winter on the Beach" Pattern Design. Adobe Illustrator and Watercolor.

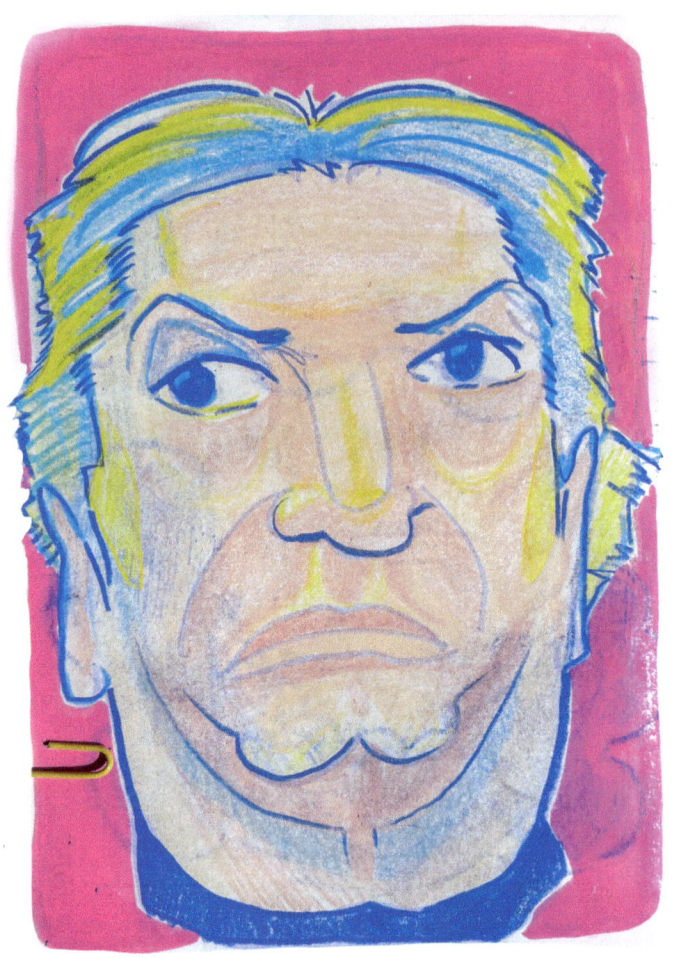
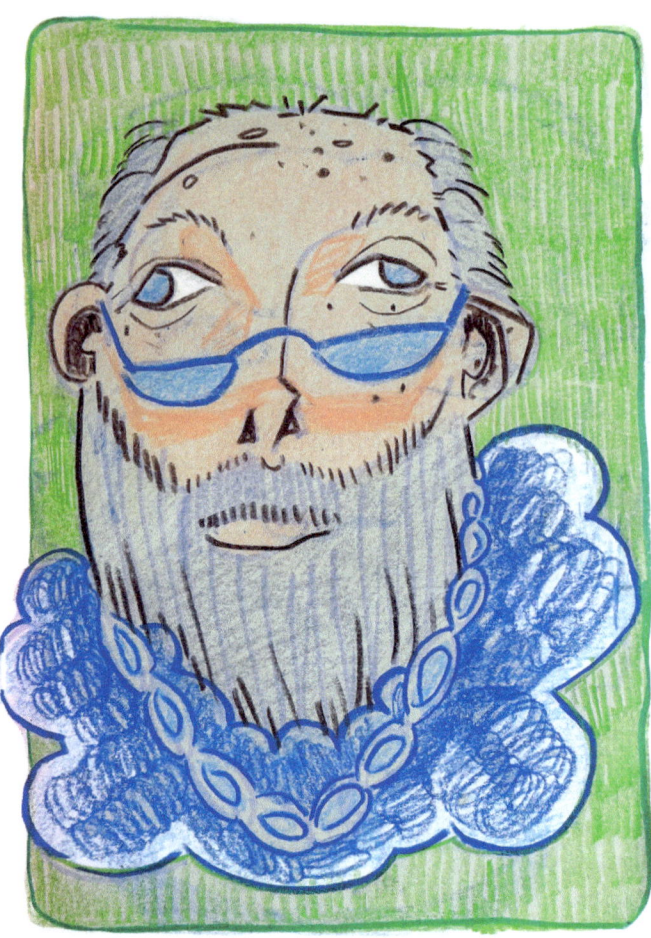
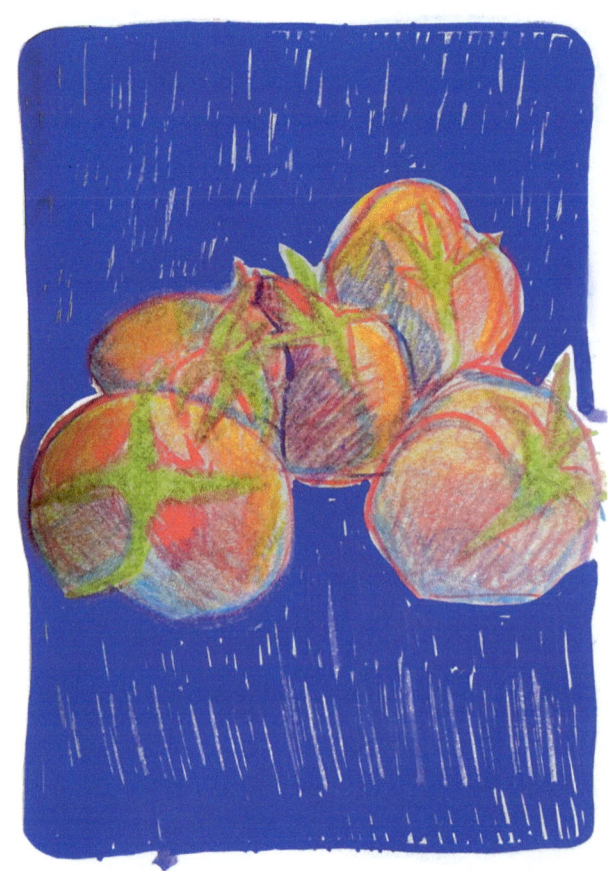

"Funky Friends" Colored Pencil. 6" x 9"

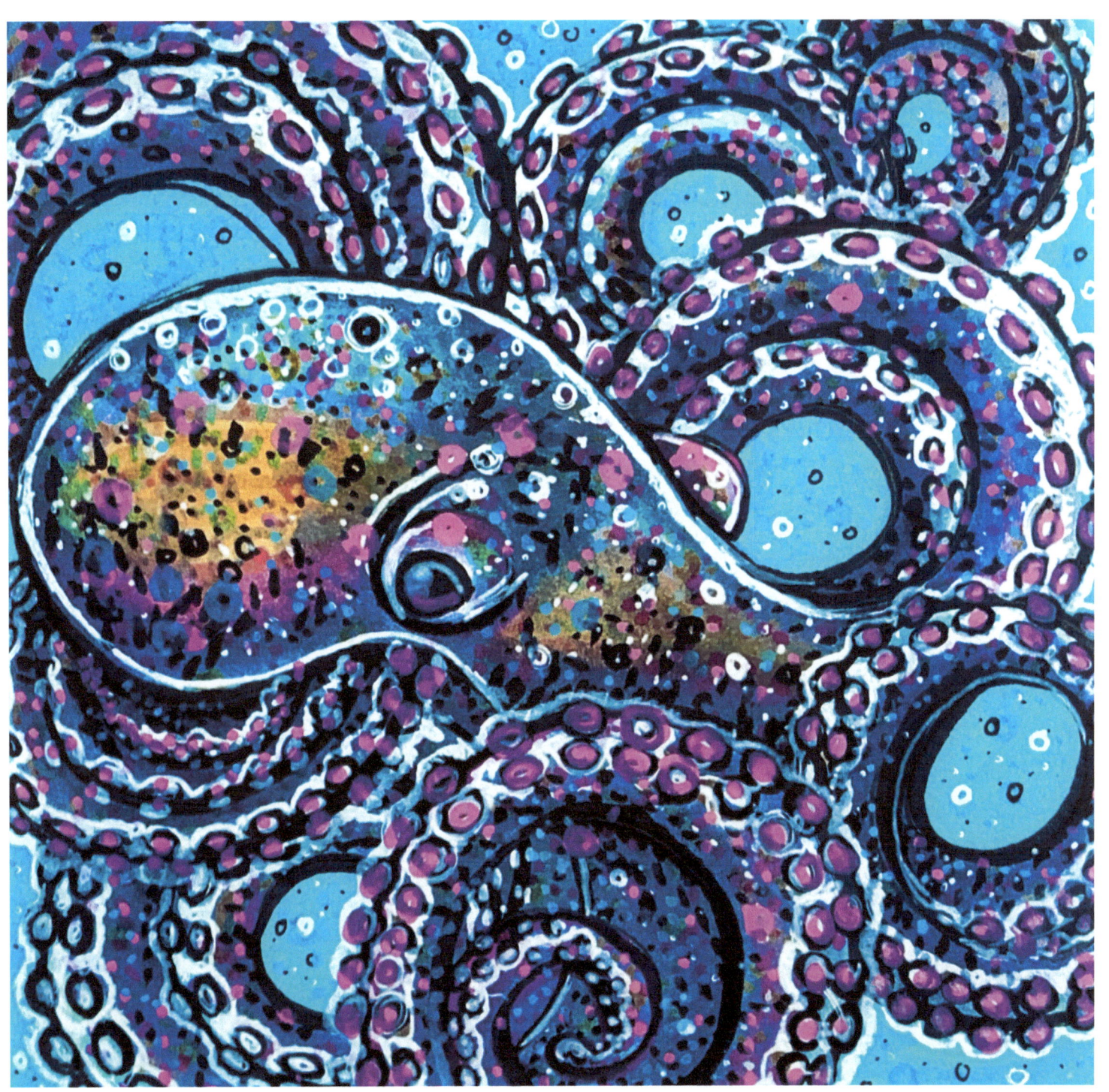

"Circles" Ink on Illustration Board. 6" x 6"

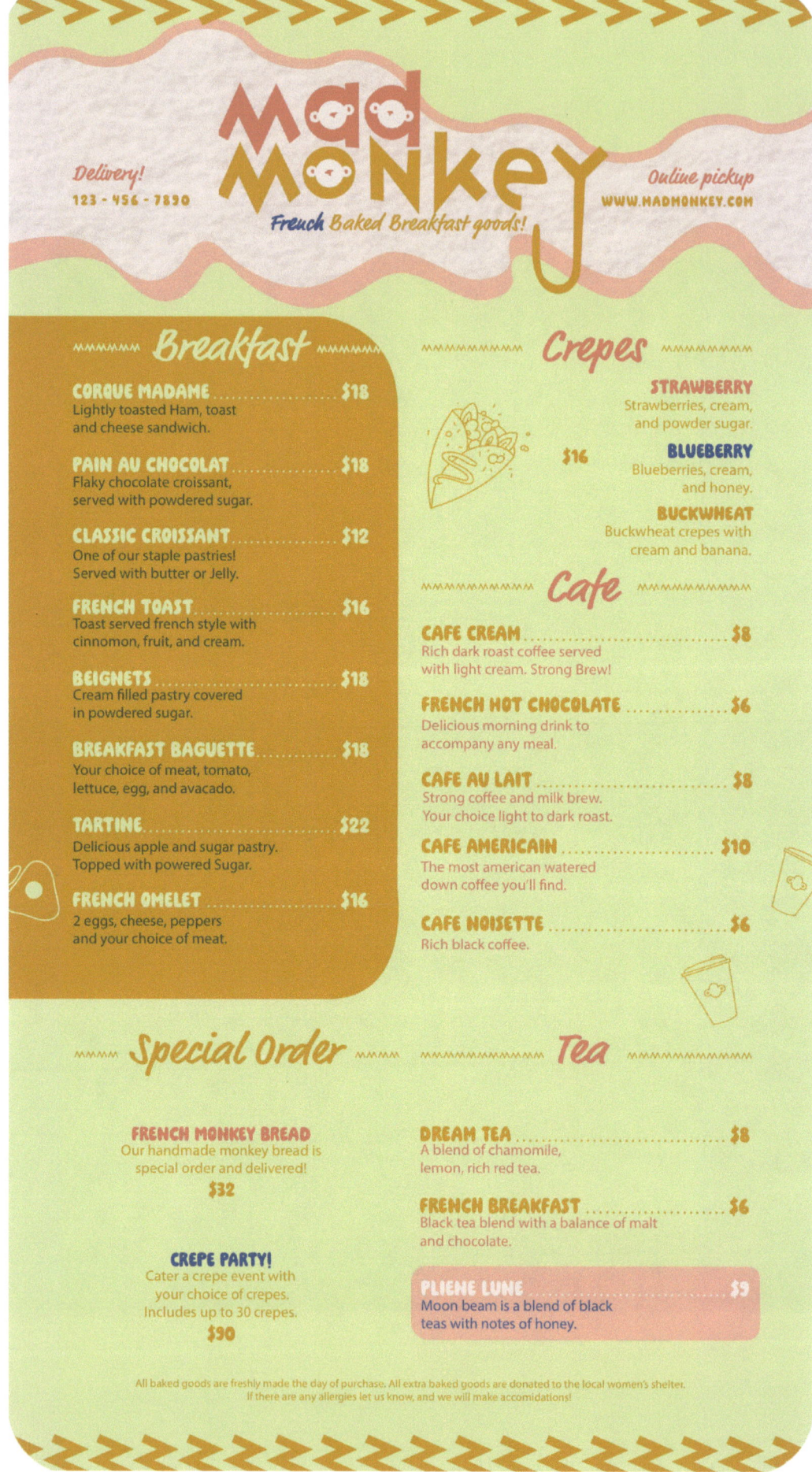

Mad Monkey Menu Mock Project. Adobe Indesign, Illustrator.

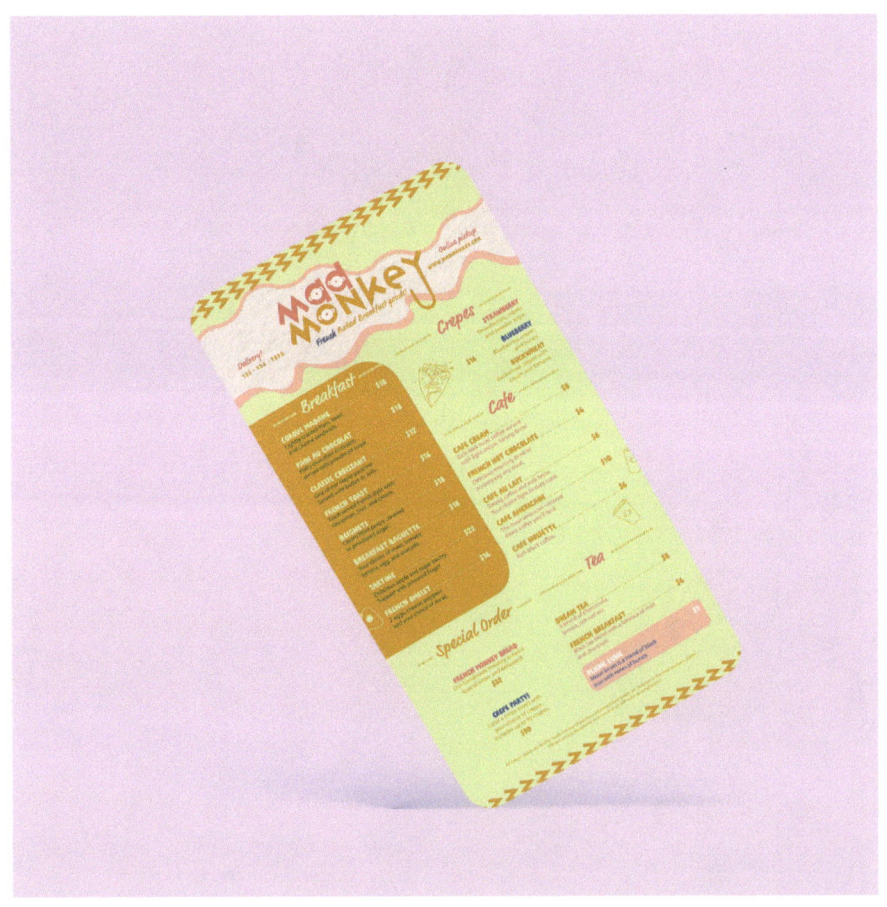
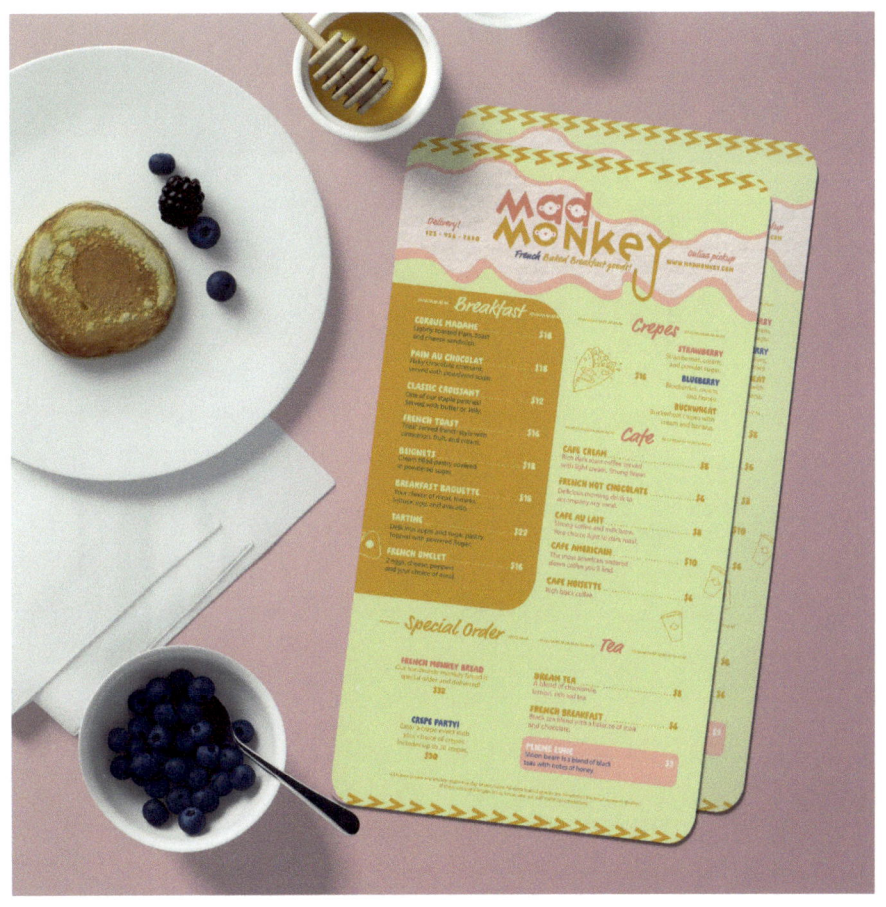

@art.with.ashlyn   www.artwithashlyn.com   artwithashlyn.co@gmail.com

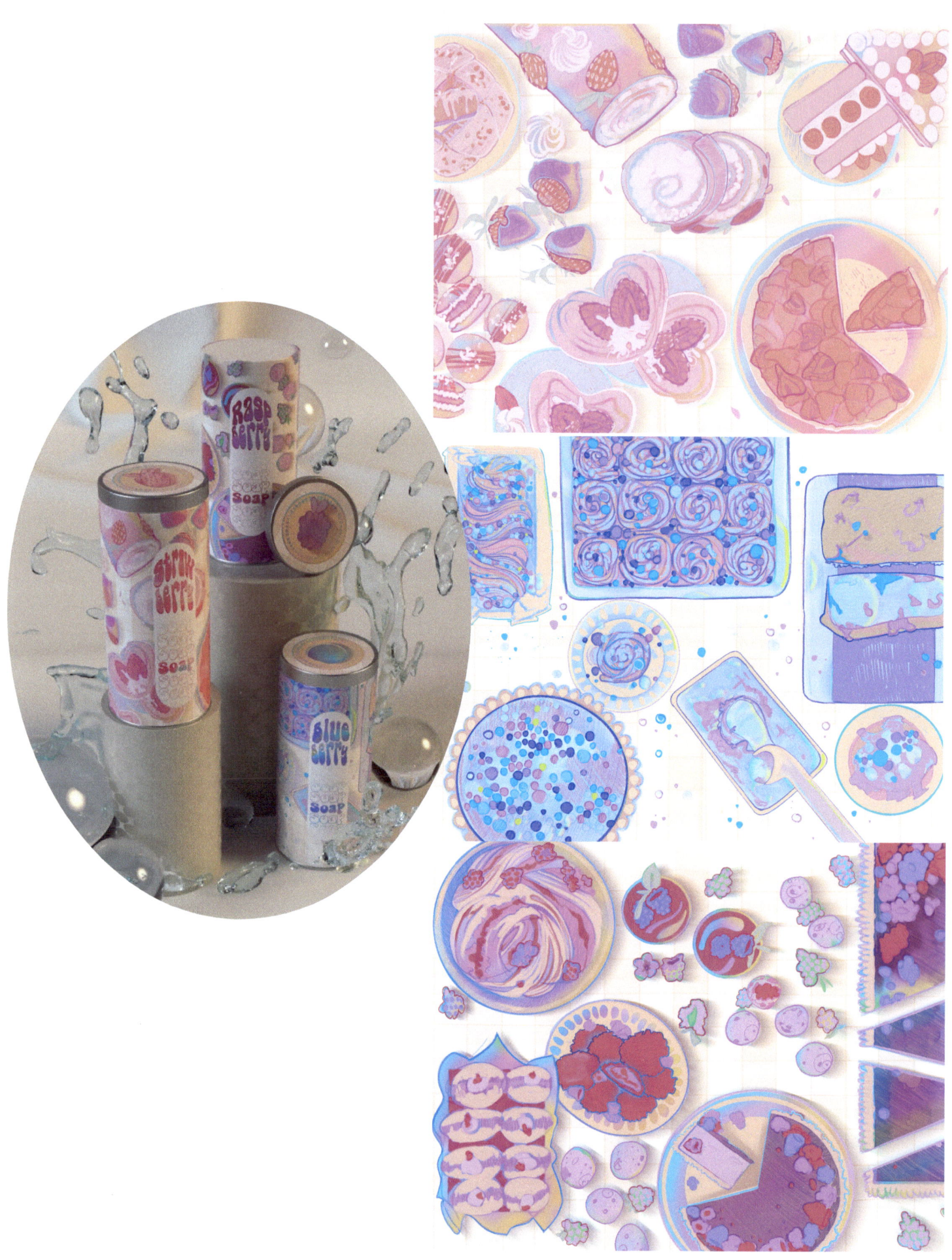

3 Tin Picnic Soap Packaging Project.

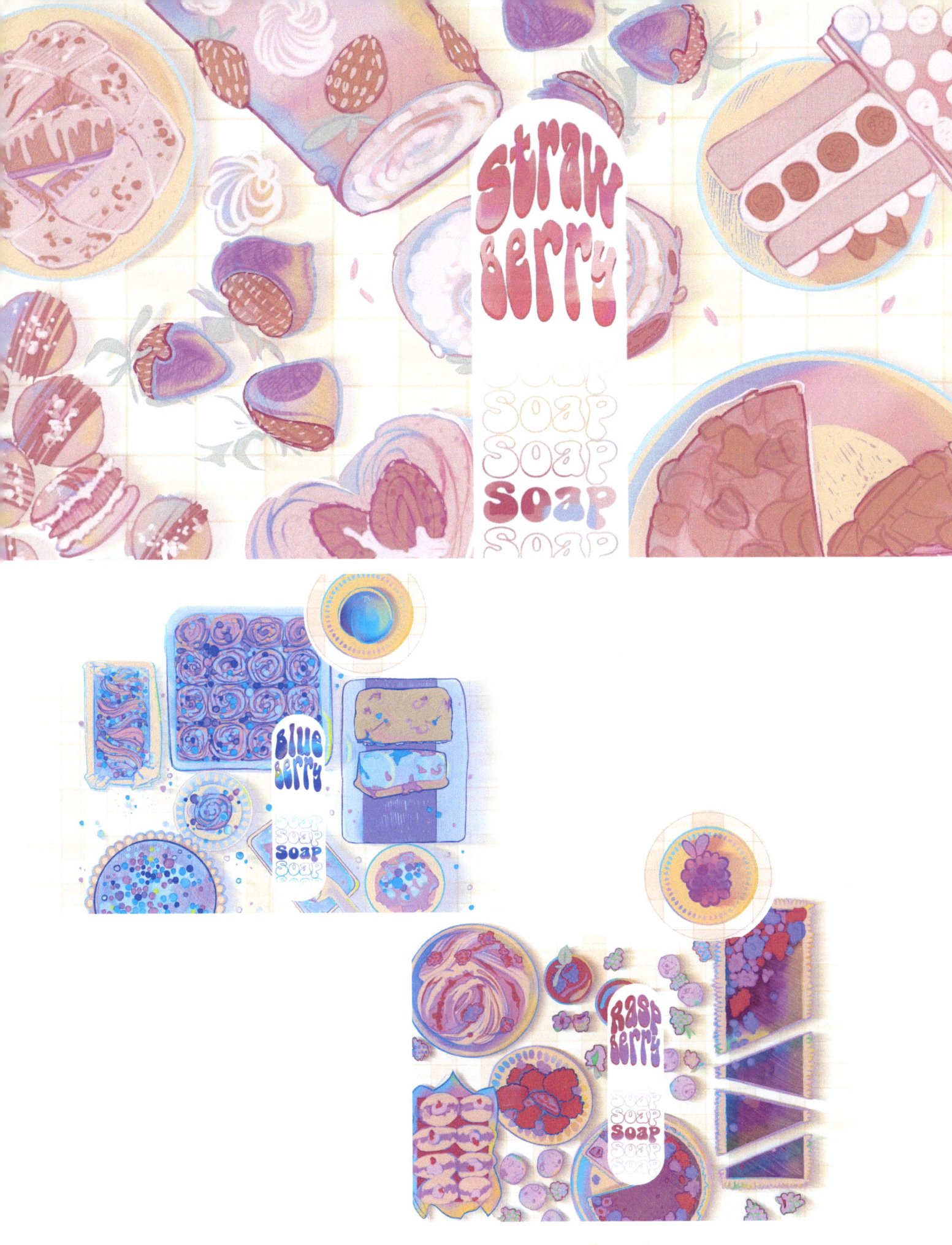

@art.with.ashlyn   www.artwithashlyn.com   artwithashlyn.co@gmail.com

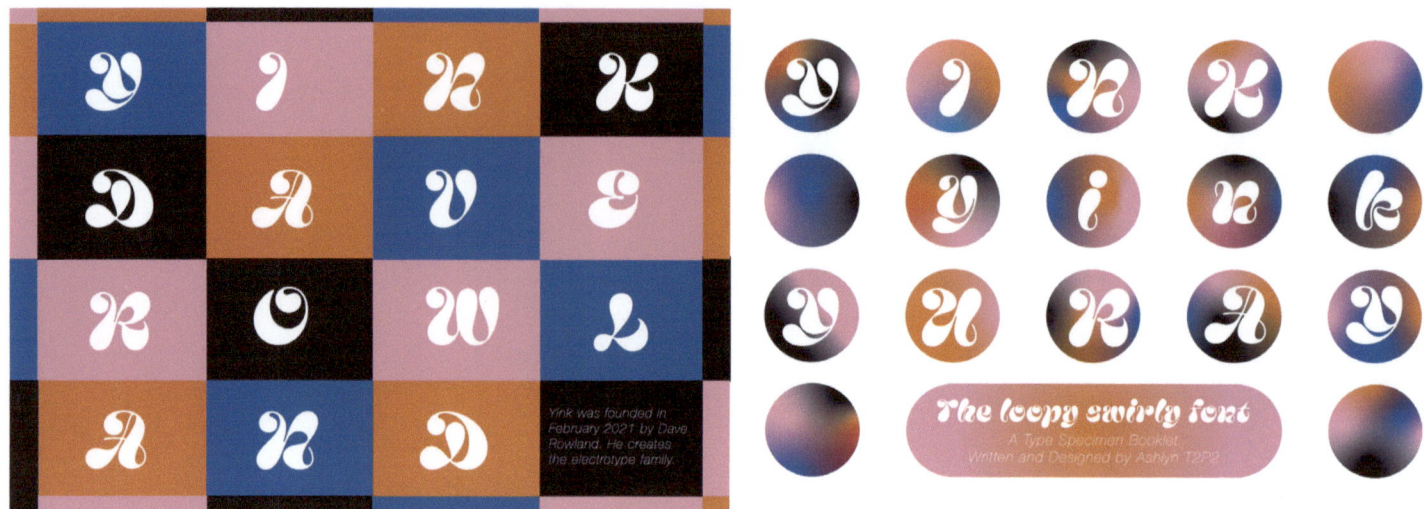

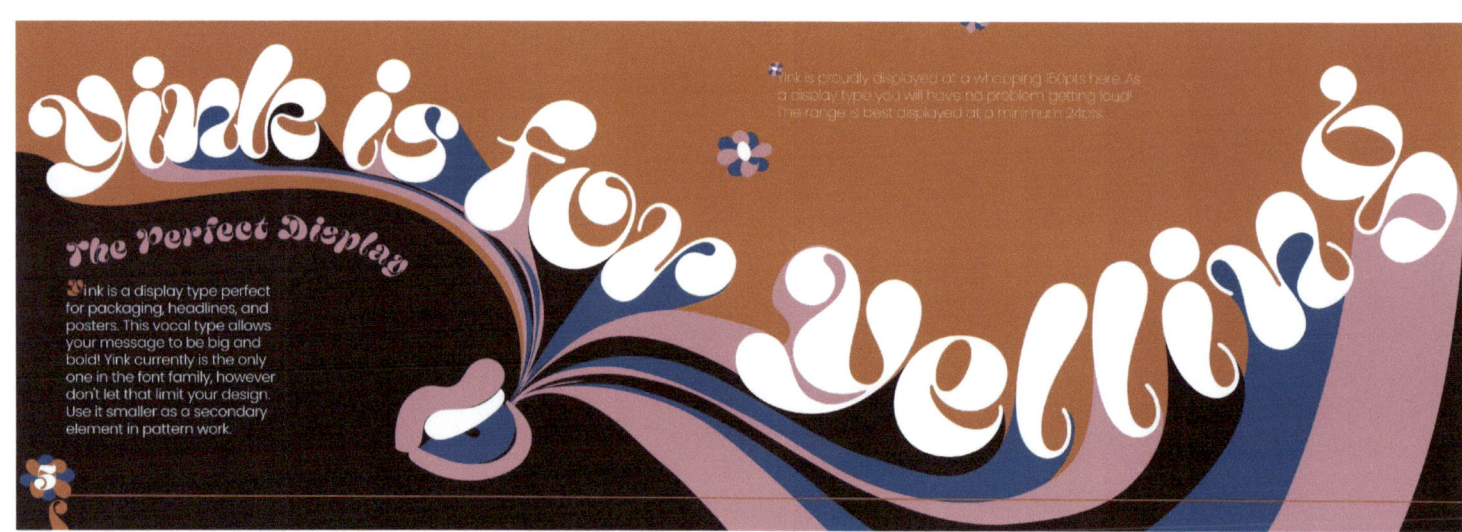

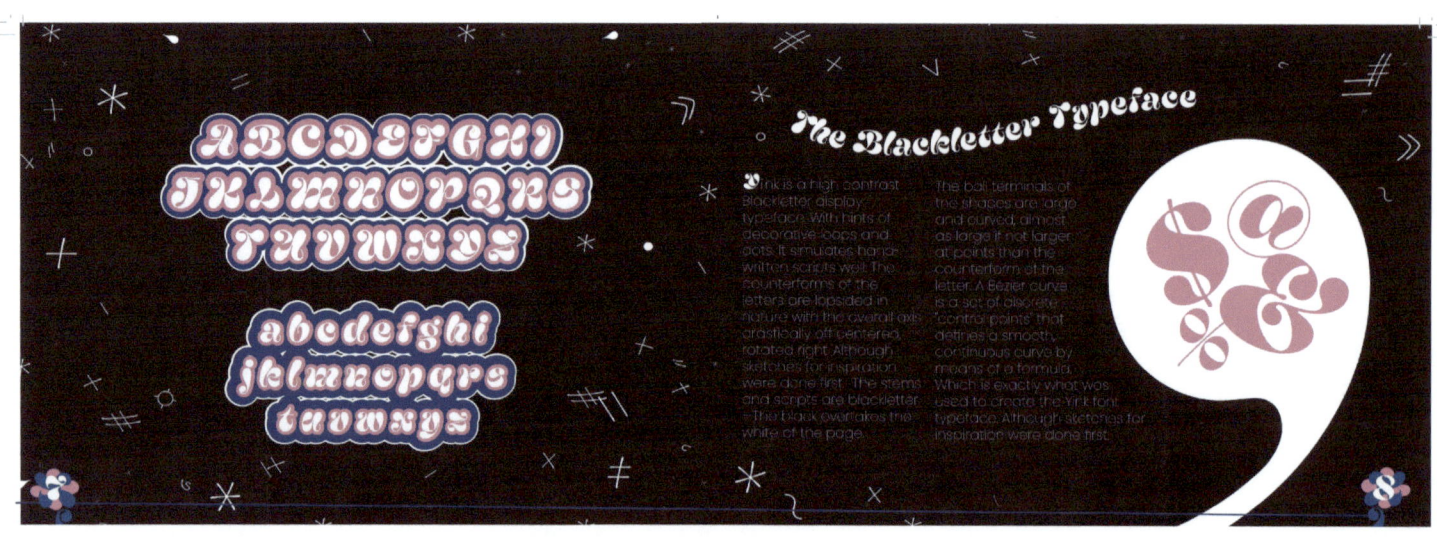

"Yink" Type Specimen Booklet. 5" x 7"

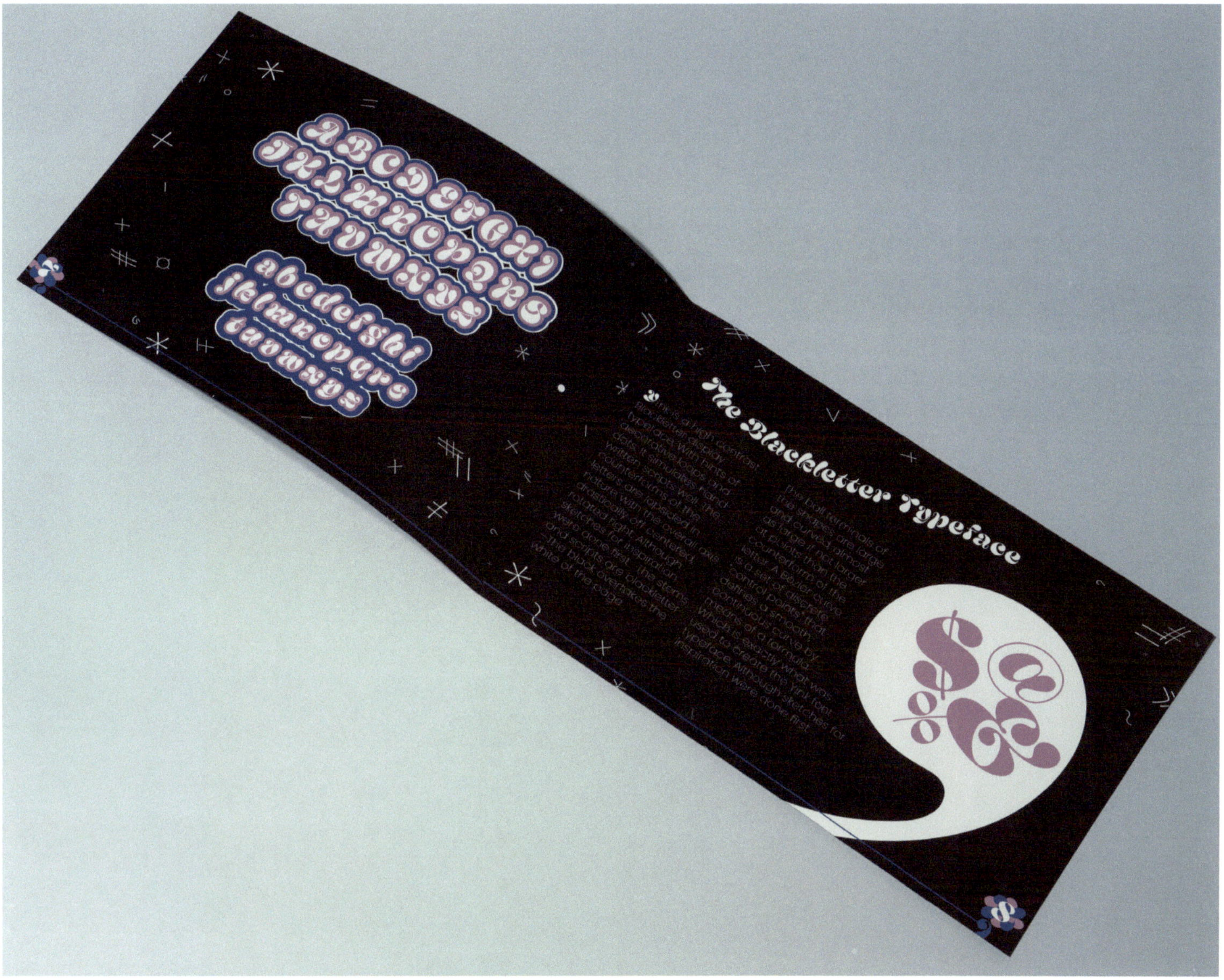

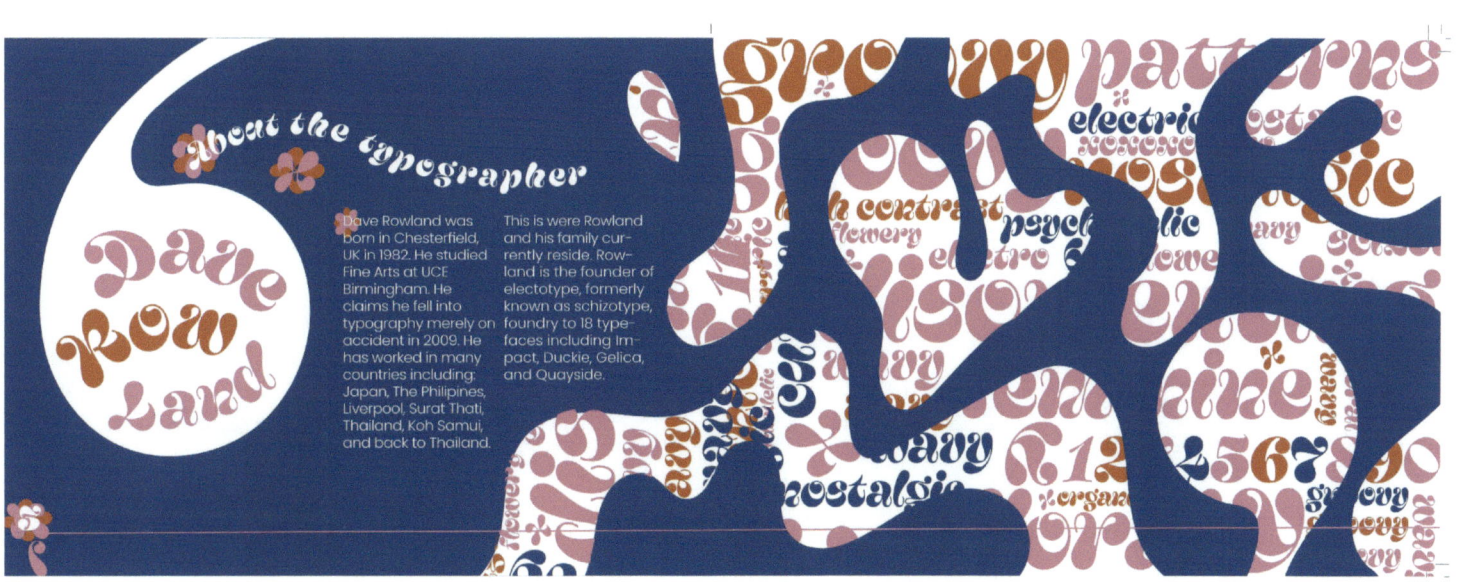

@art.with.ashlyn   www.artwithashlyn.com   artwithashlyn.co@gmail.com

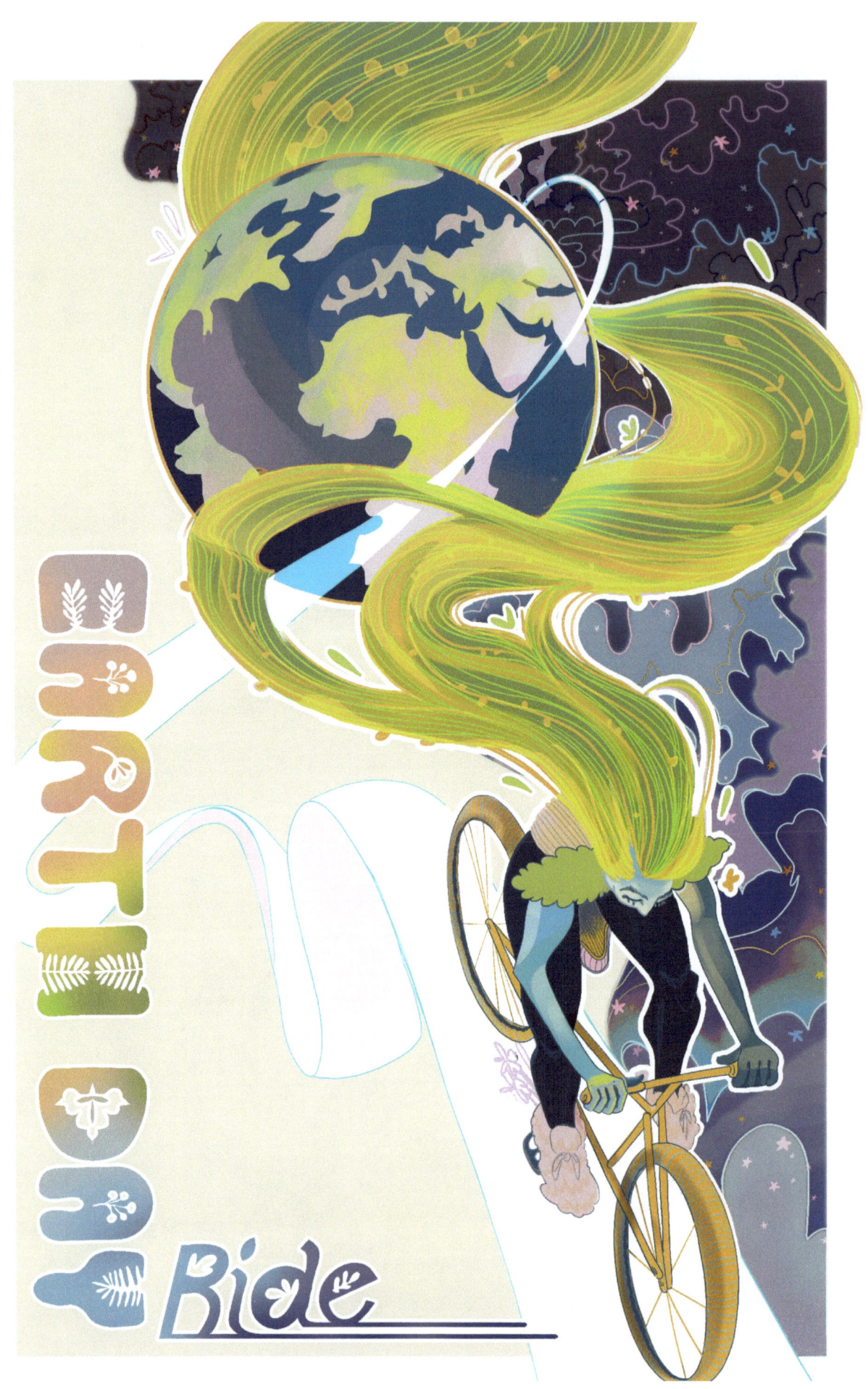

"Earth Day Ride" Poster. Adobe Photoshop. 24" x 36"

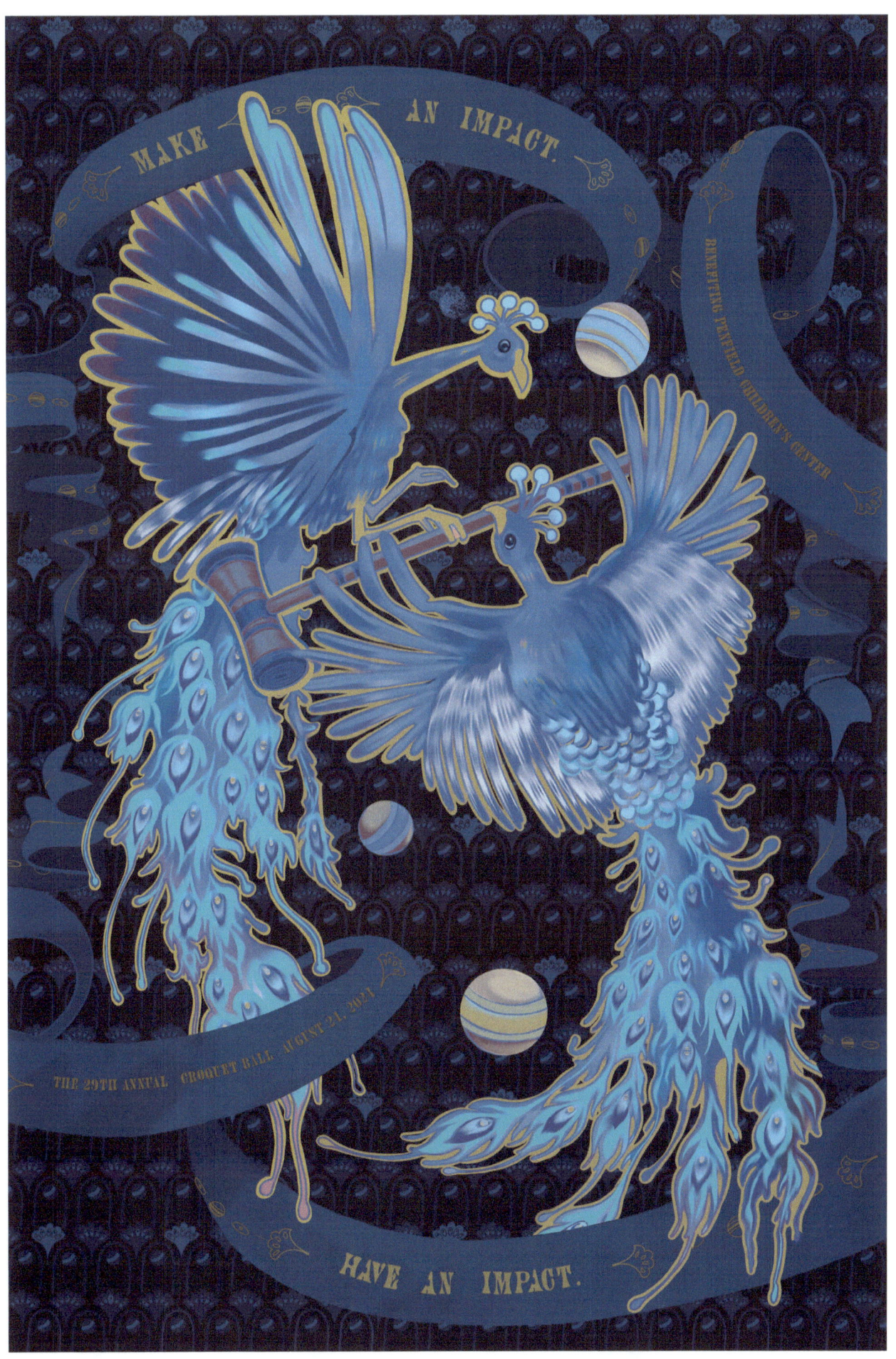

"Make and Impact Have an Impact" Poster. Adobe Photoshop. 26" x 40'

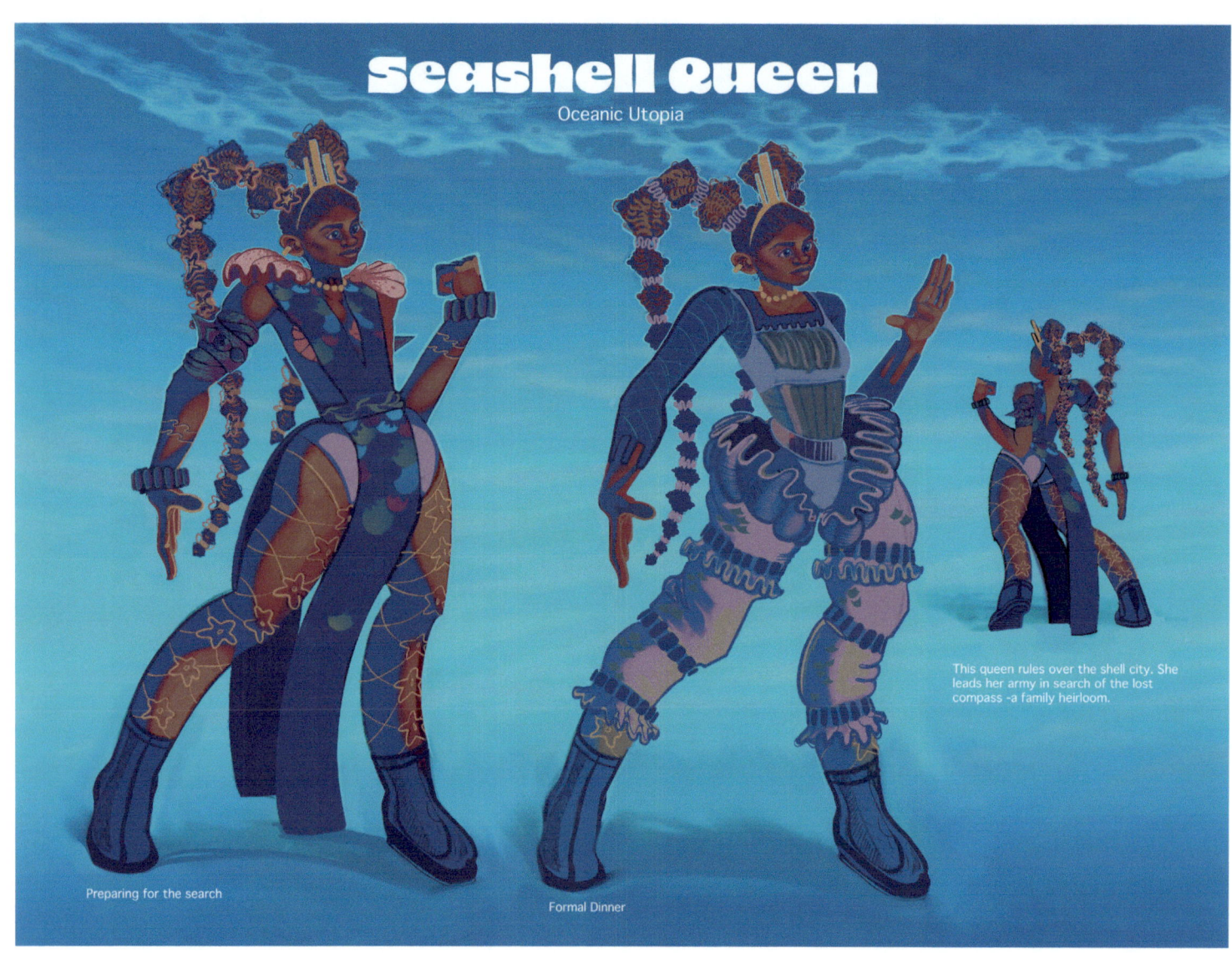

Concept Ocean Character Design.

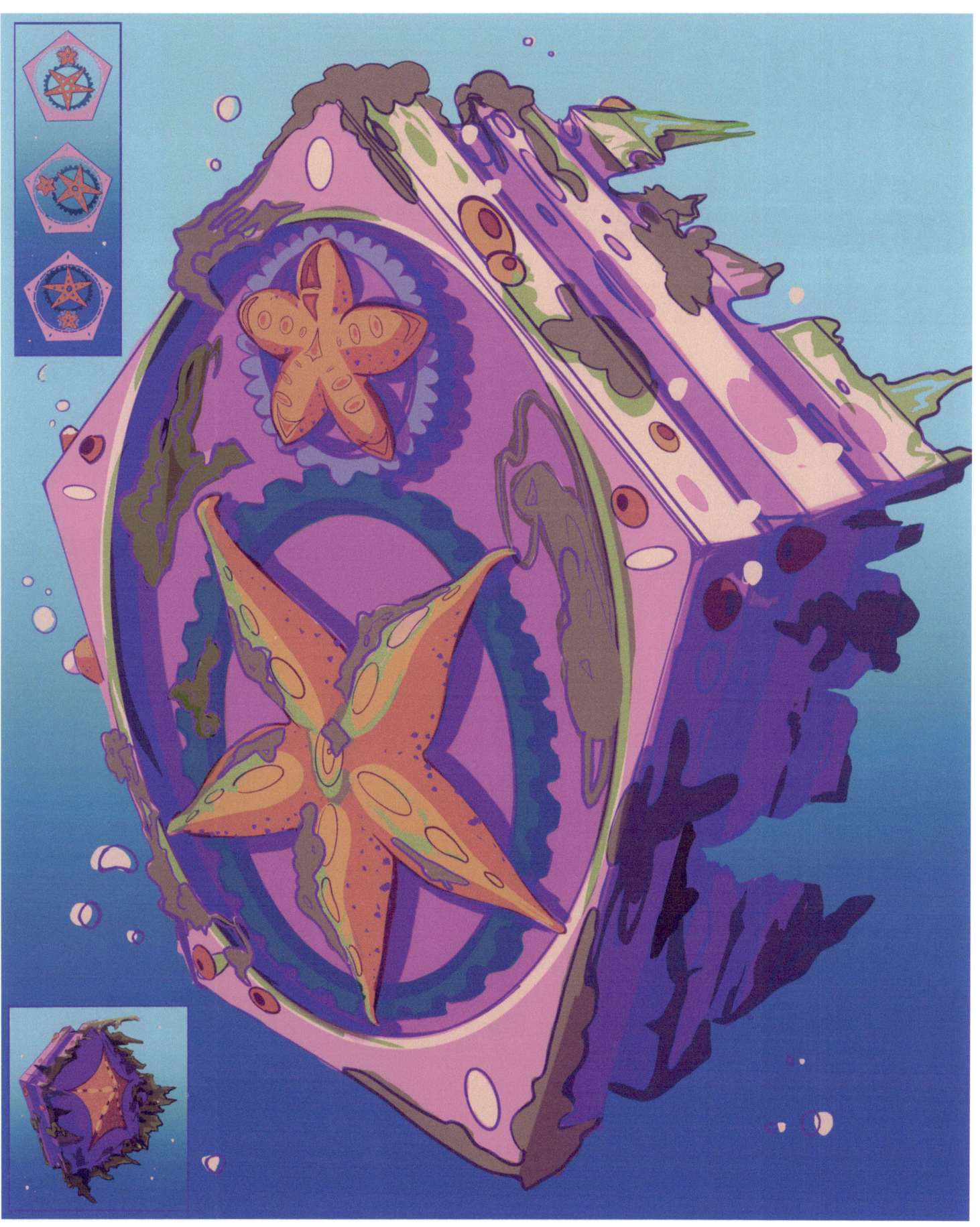

Concept Ocean Seastar Compass.

LOTUS

UNTOLD STORIES

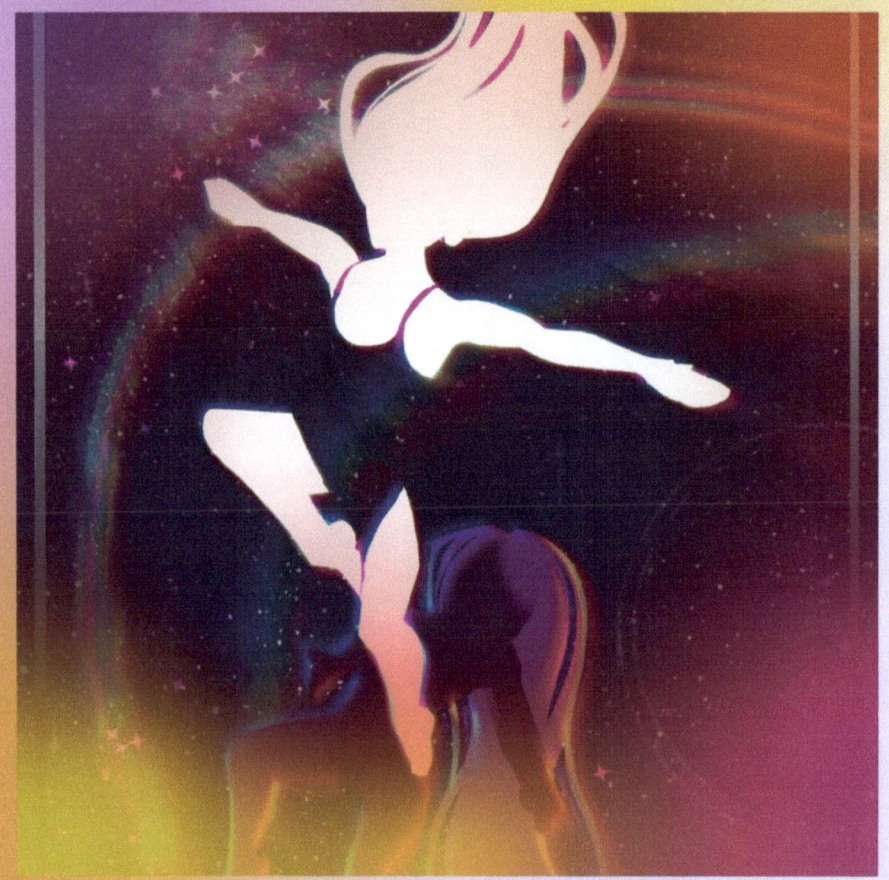

ISSUE 6 | 2024

"Untold Stories" Issue 6 Response Artwork. Lotus Legal Clinic.

Hidden Blessing
Ashley Suttle

I remember laying sedated on a hospital bed. Angry and sad.
Starring into the dark hollow eyes of the officer dispatched
to question my sanity.
I remember having the enemy of my enemy kick in my door
to save my life only to further tarnish and make dim
my soul of drowning light.
I remember that day in September when I regressed in meditation,
asking God to show me what it was about me that attracted you.
I remember drifting into the void as the images of my uncle
flashed upon mind between the basement and the water bed.
I remember the movie reel of many lives
including my own daughter flooding my mind
exposing the shared trauma.
In my mind I went crazy saying, "No, not my daughter!"
I remember the backlash, the slander, the gossip, the gaslighting
between you and my family who did nothing
even when I was a child.
I remember in September sitting with grandmother's medicine
in a field with other beacons trying to grasp for purpose.
Every moon cycle, through every upgrade of consciousness,
I climbed the mountains reaching…
reaching for the light.
I rose above it all after every attack sent to my spirit
that felt like lashes of fire being burned into my skin.
The little girl inside of me screamed louder than a death whistle
on a foggy night in darkness, left to die.
They were wrong, every last one of them.
I realize that after every blow of pressure I became
a red diamond of cosmic power.
A being birthed from many creeds.
Protected.

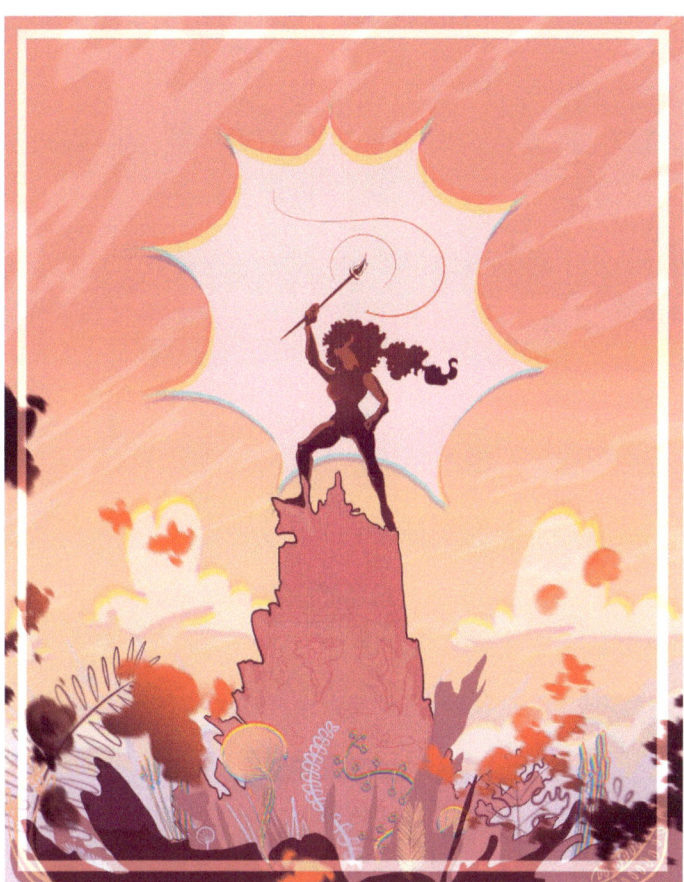

Ashlyn Bledsoe

Galaxy Girl
Nao mi

I met a mystical fairy named Galaxy Girl.
She inspires the world and defeats mediocracy.
Few understand how she does it
but it's the way she loses herself in every art,
the way she catches on and masters with skill
like poetry in a crafted body,
the satisfying of words falling from hydrated lips,
a psalm of verses that desperately have you dying
to read and stay in bed.
Like the ripping at the edges of a masterpiece
she pieced her peace together.
It's the way her dragon-fire passion skulled you
with inspiring temptation,
a new rescuing sensation that was beautifully excruciating,
a flame bright enough to disturb the solar system
and intermission the sky to defeat fearful thoughts that demise.
She burned like a collapsing shower of stars.
She would always give a ton of Jupiter's love,
the most beautiful cosmos and Milky Way reruns,
the most inferior bee sting of relief.
She carried a moon-dusted heart and star-dusted
ambers in her hands, the tree of life in her hair
and feet full of fun. She shimmered of light
because of the darkness she overcame
and that glow was enough to awaken the sun.
She hopes that you remember
the planetary battles you've won
and continue to see the grace
in your unspoken song.

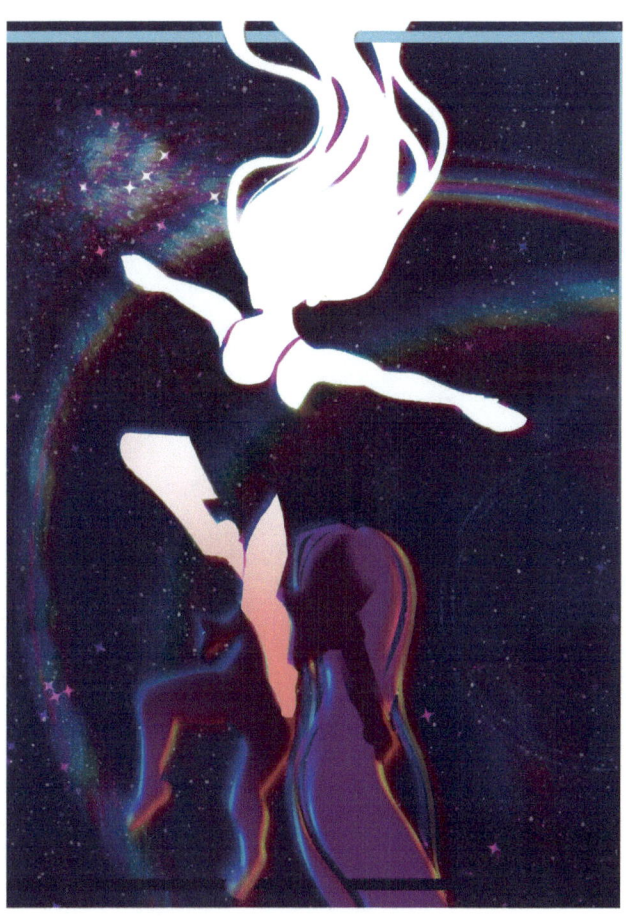

Ashlyn Bledsoe

@art.with.ashlyn   www.artwithashlyn.com   artwithashlyn.co@gmail.com

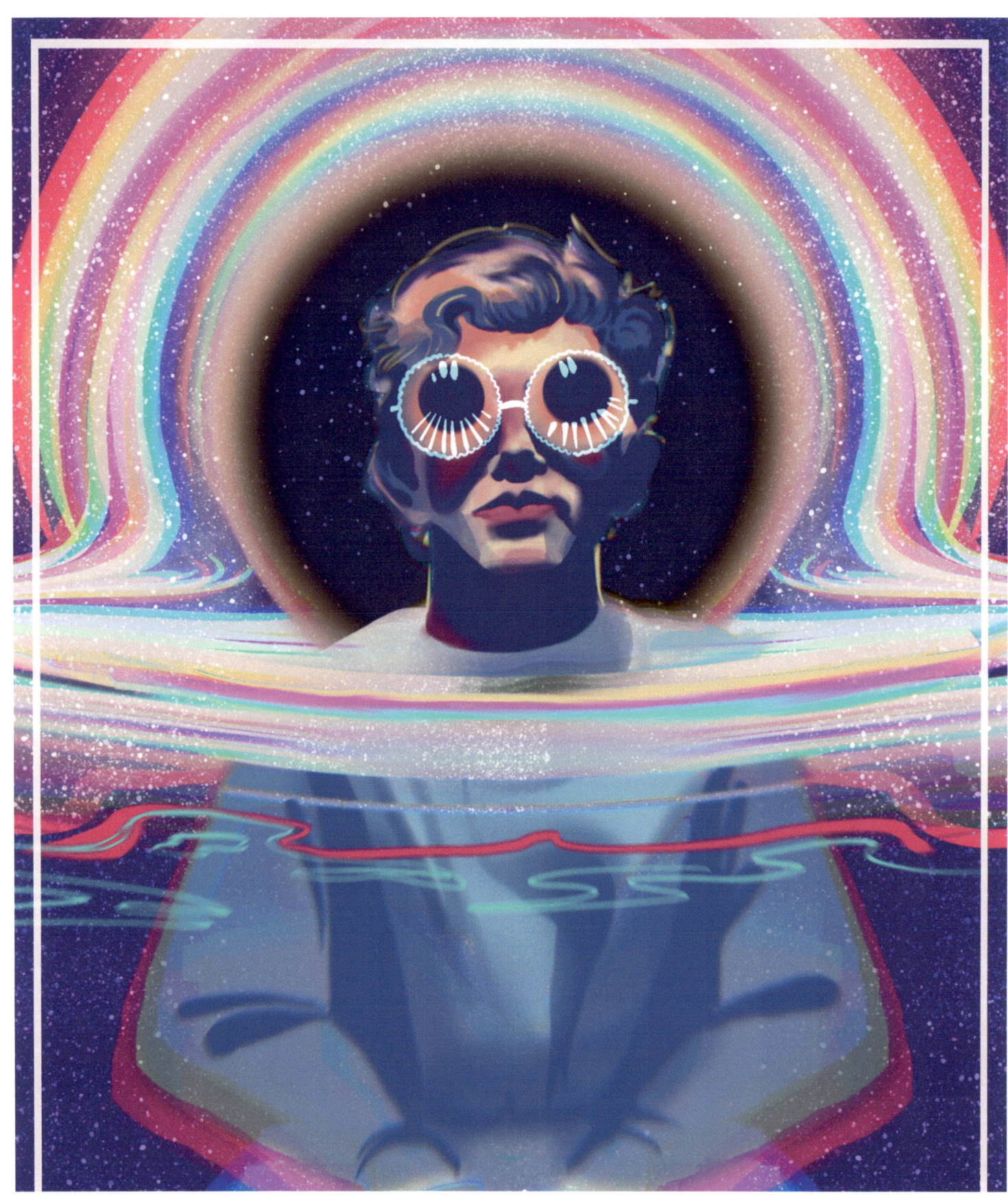
"Galaxy Boy" Portrait 6/100.

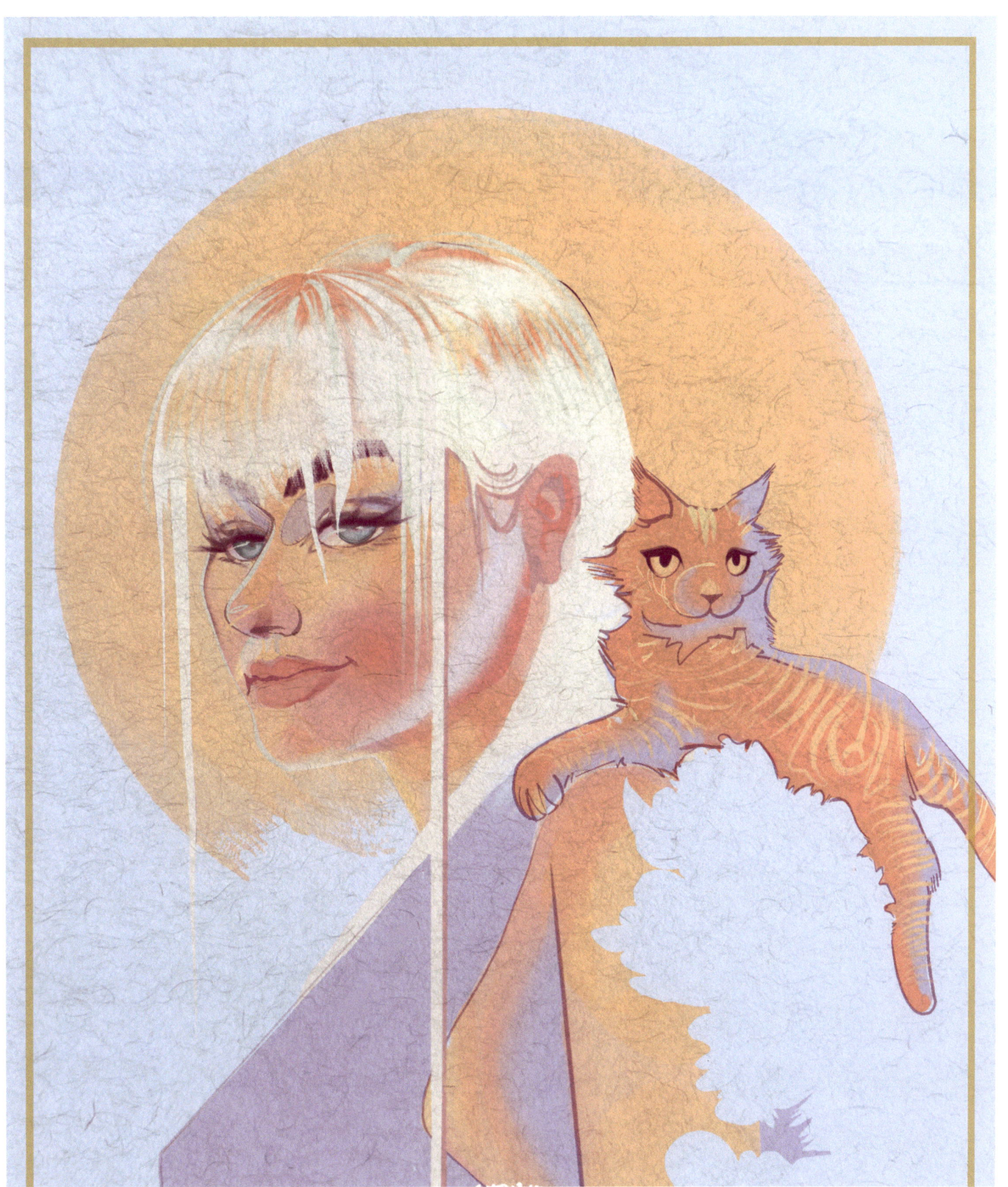

"Miso Soup" Portrait 3/100.

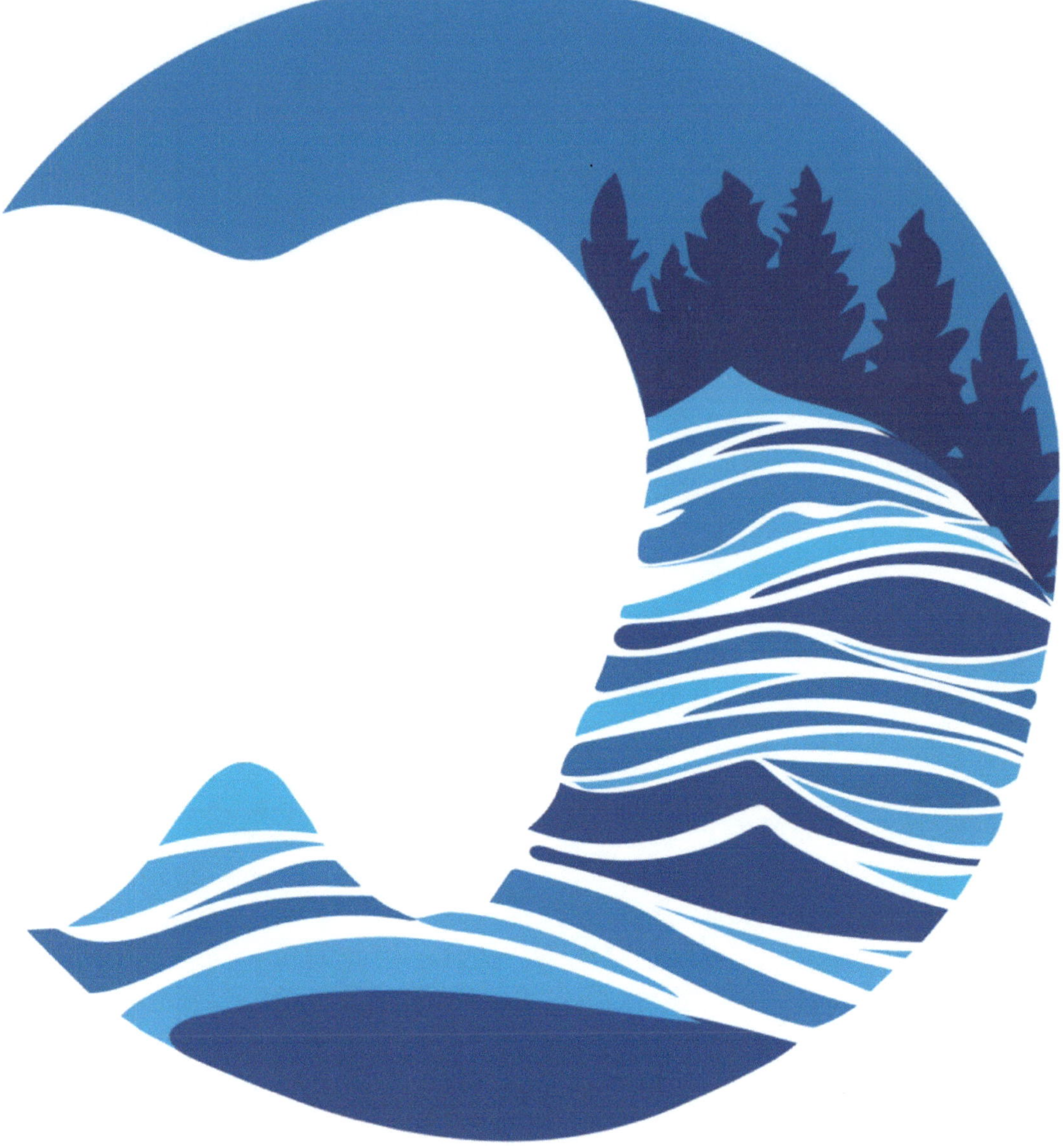

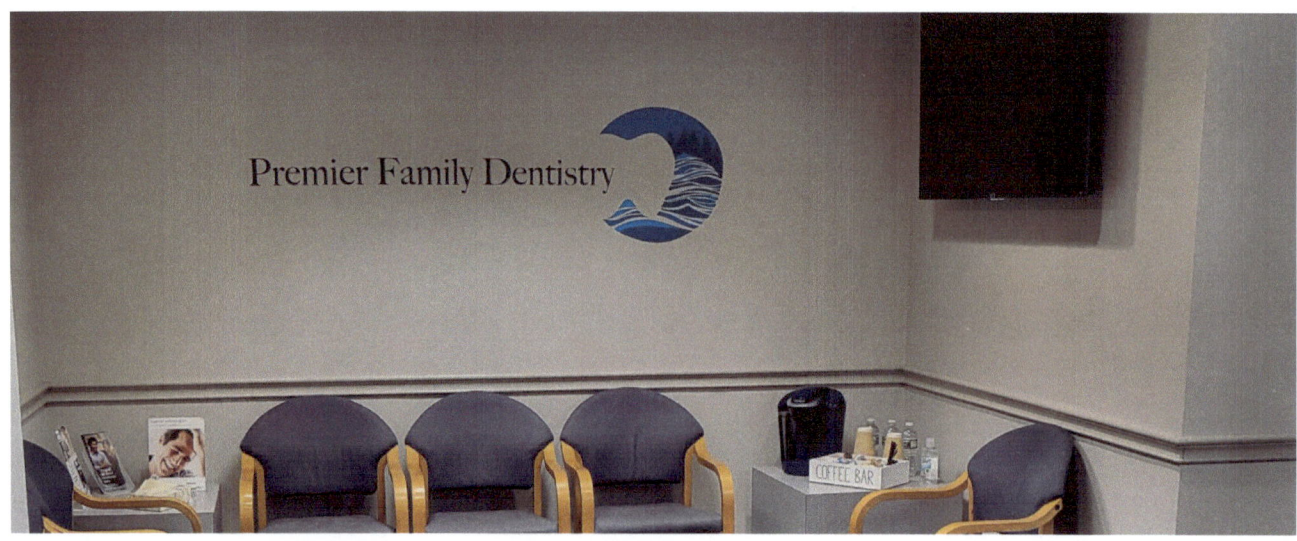

Premier Family Dentistry, Brand Identity. Adobe Illustrator.

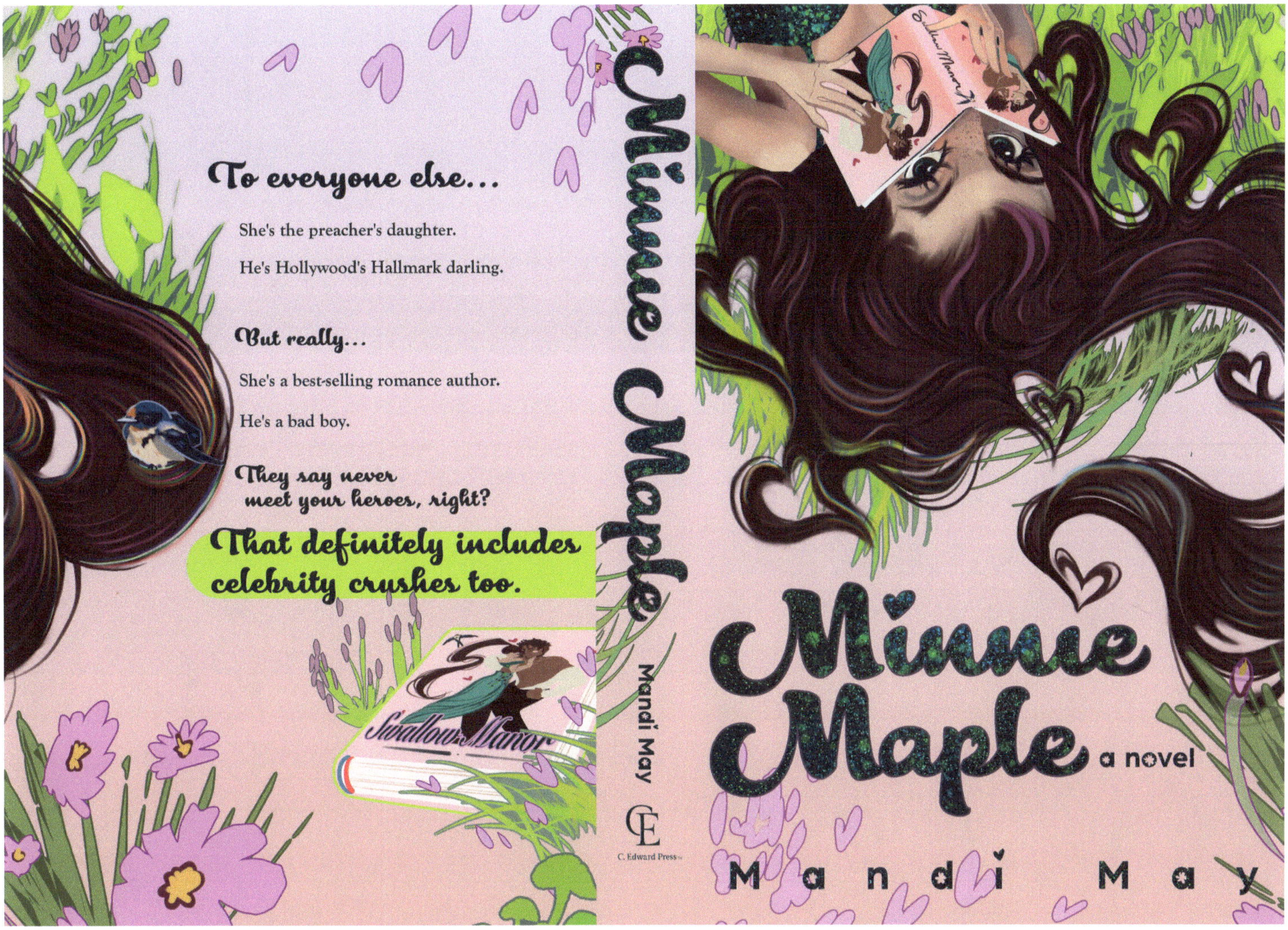

To everyone else...
She's the preacher's daughter.
He's Hollywood's Hallmark darling.

But really...
She's a best-selling romance author.
He's a bad boy.

They say never meet your heroes, right?
That definitely includes celebrity crushes too.

Minnie Maple
a novel

Mandi May

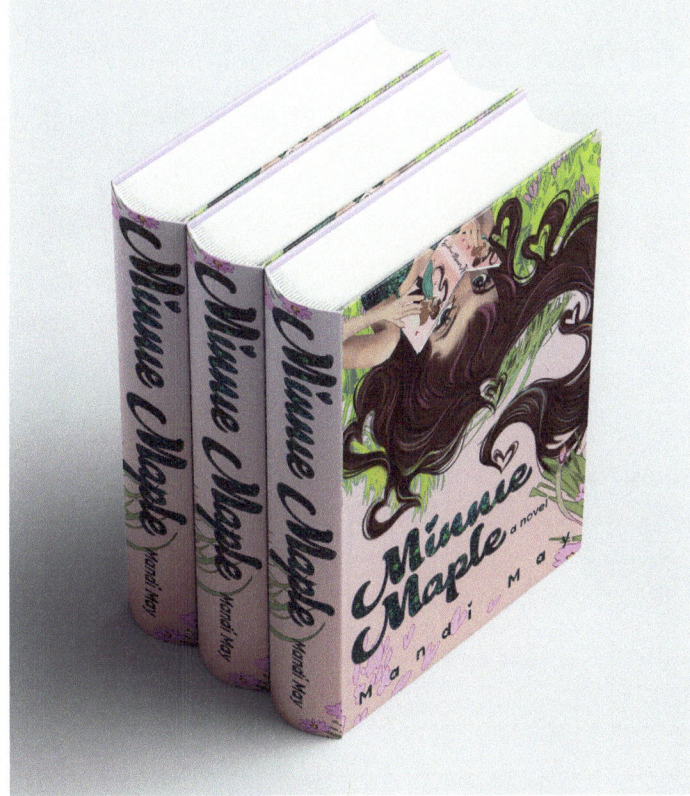
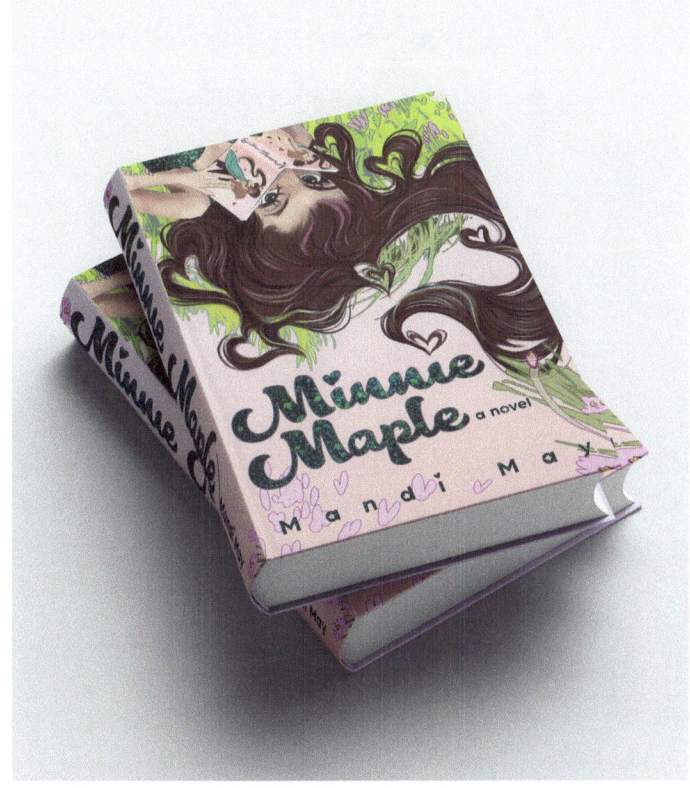

"Minnie Maple" Book Cover Illustration & Design. Adobe Photoshop. 6" x 9"

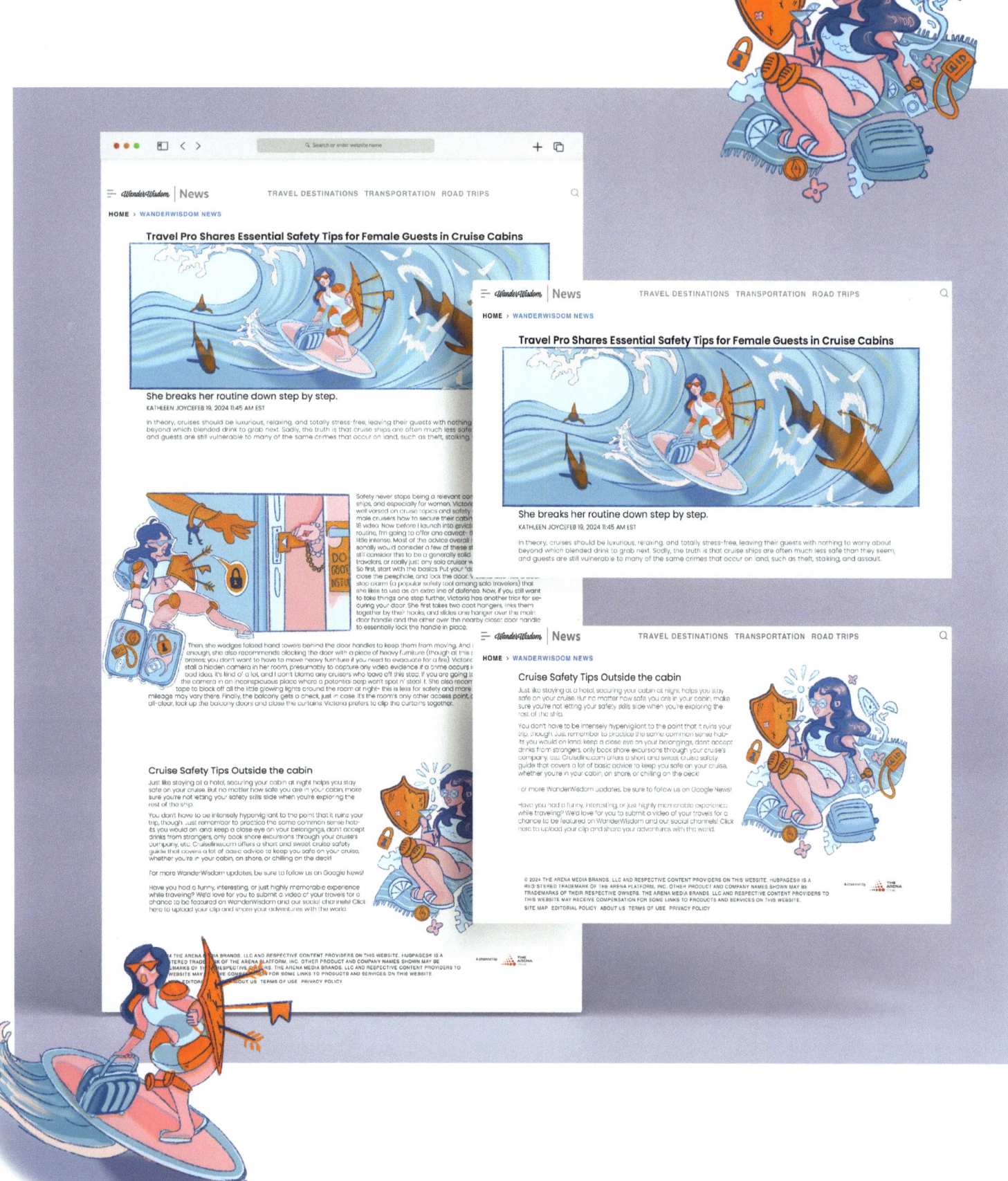

Cruise Cabin Editorial Mock Project.

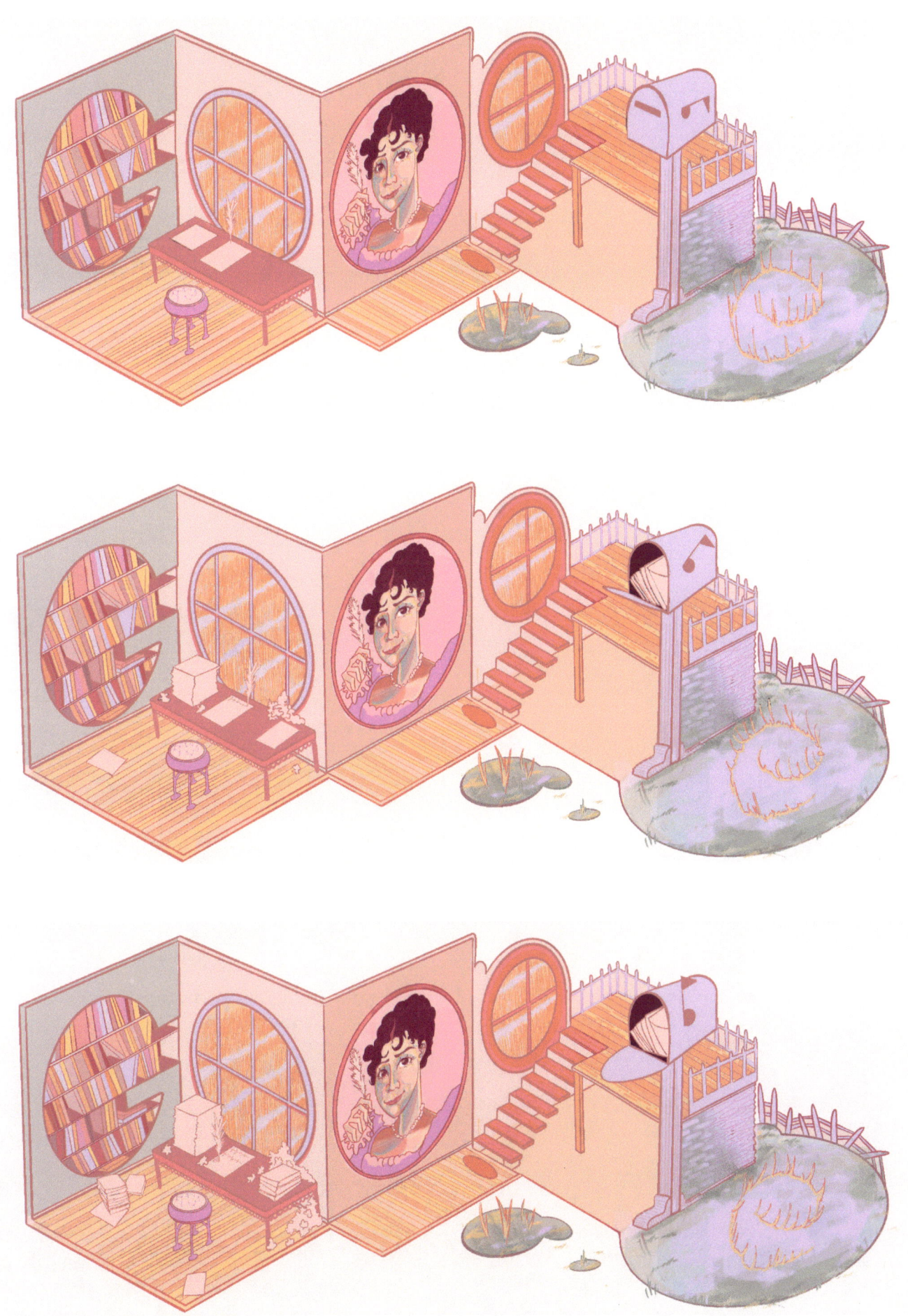

"Google Doodle" of Jane Austen .GIF

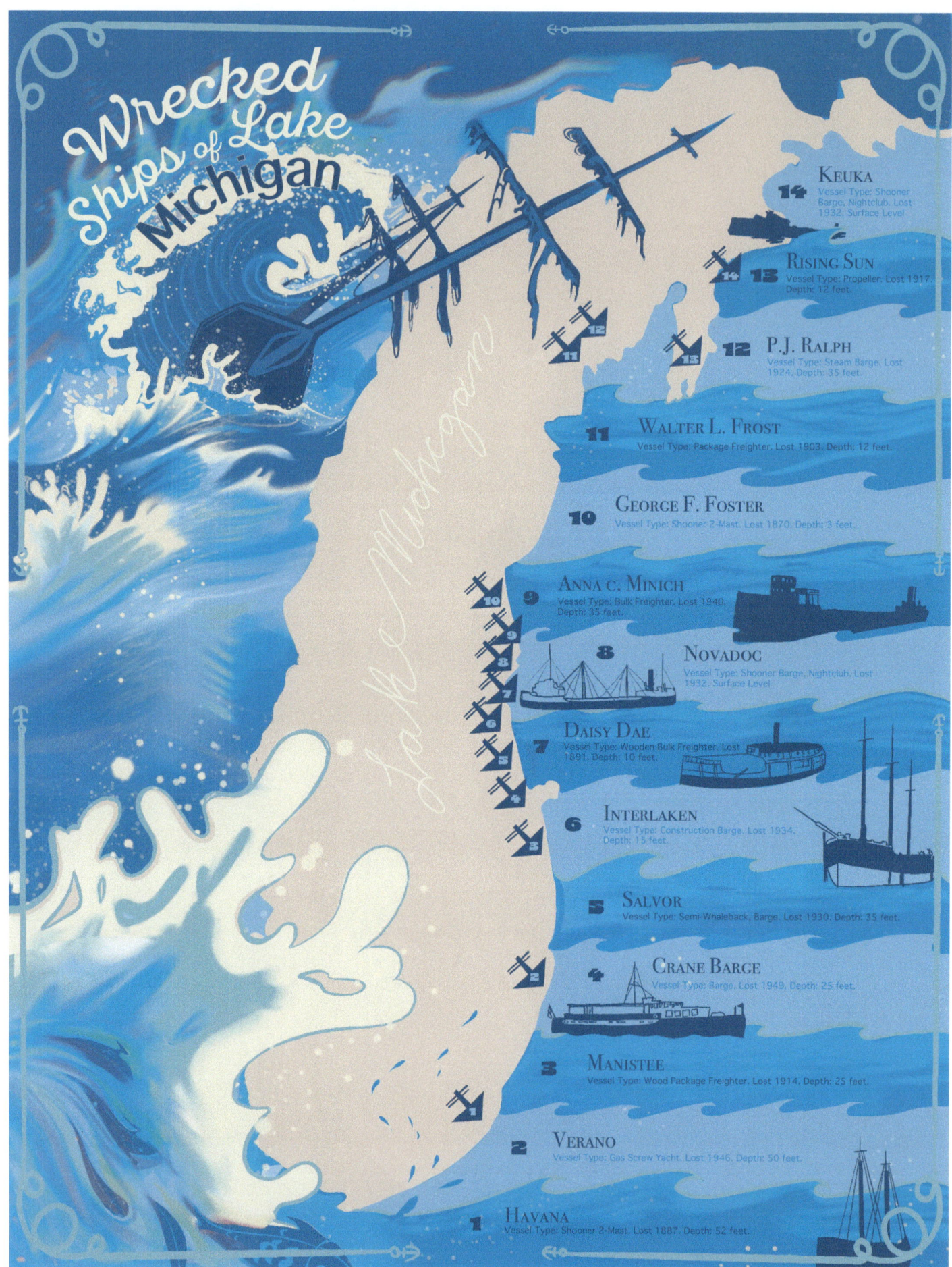

Maps of Shipwrecks in Lake Michigan.

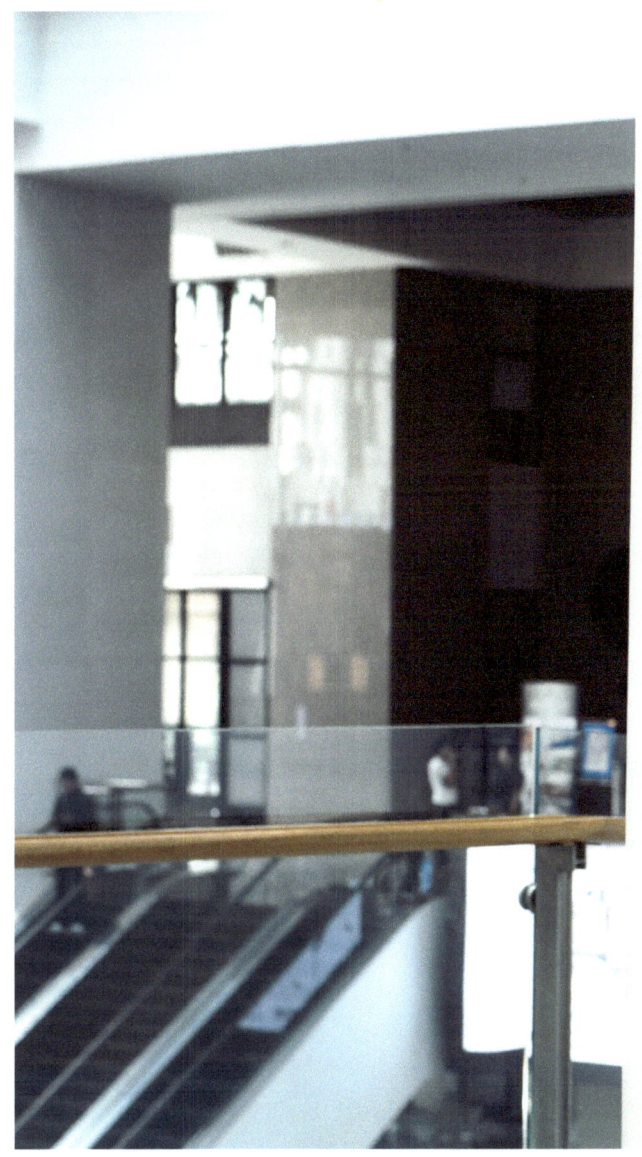
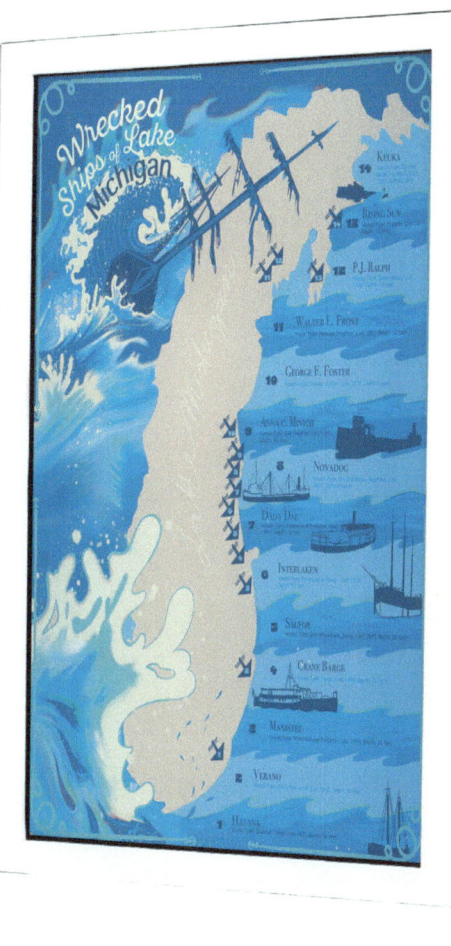

@art.with.ashlyn   www.artwithashlyn.com   artwithashlyn.co@gmail.com

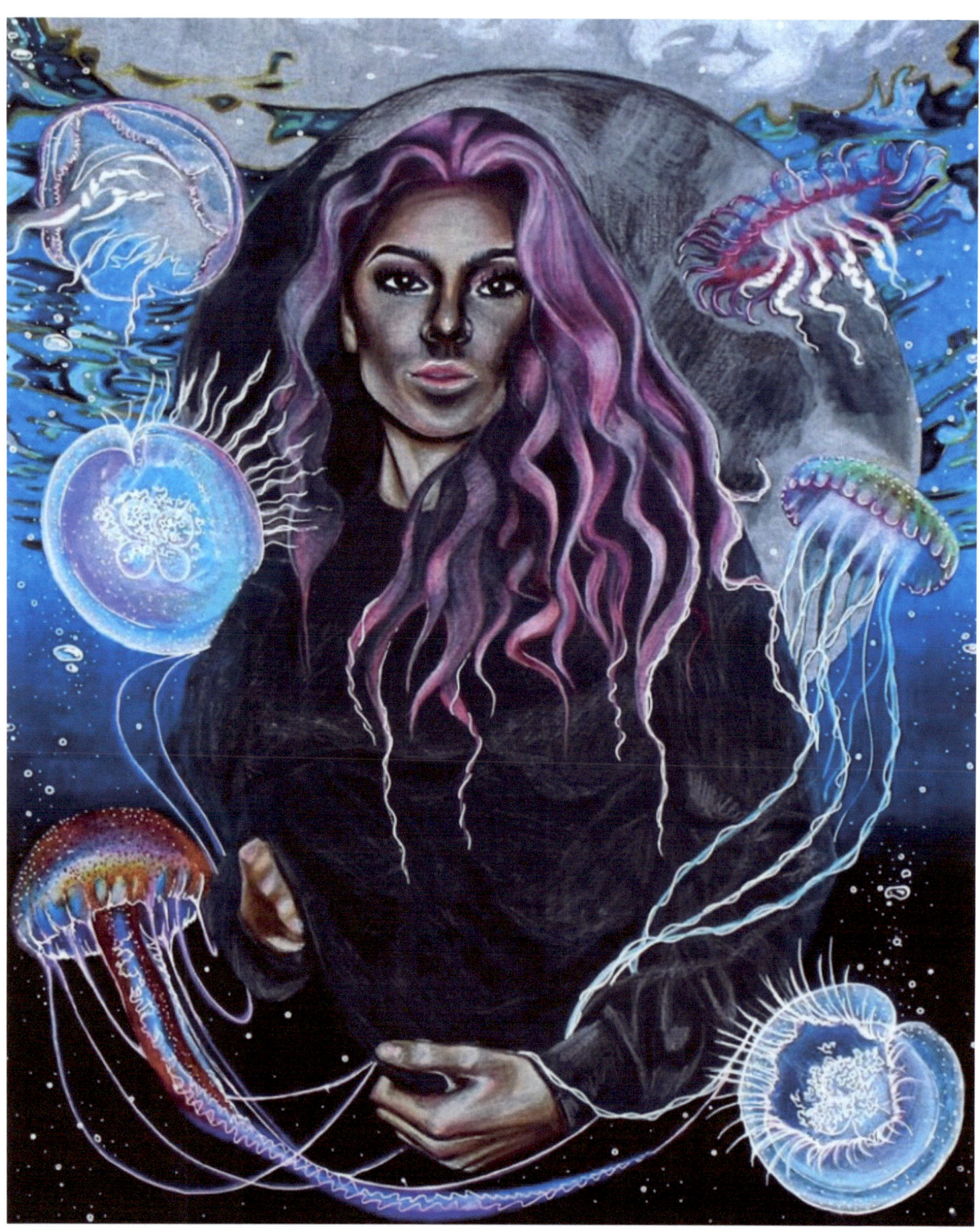

"Jelly Moon Woman" Colored Pencil. 24" x 36"

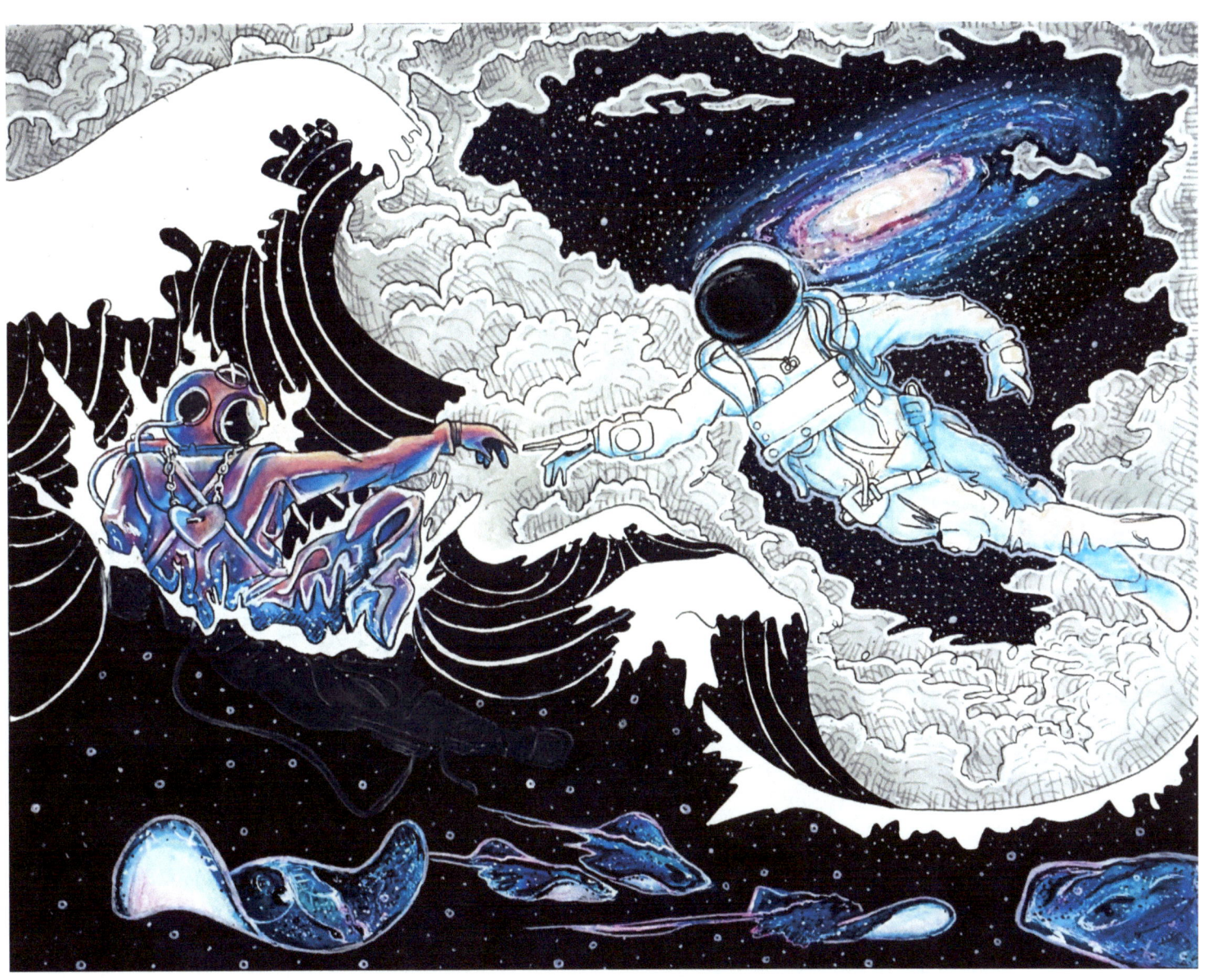

"The great wave x Space" Ink on Illustration Board. 10" x 12"

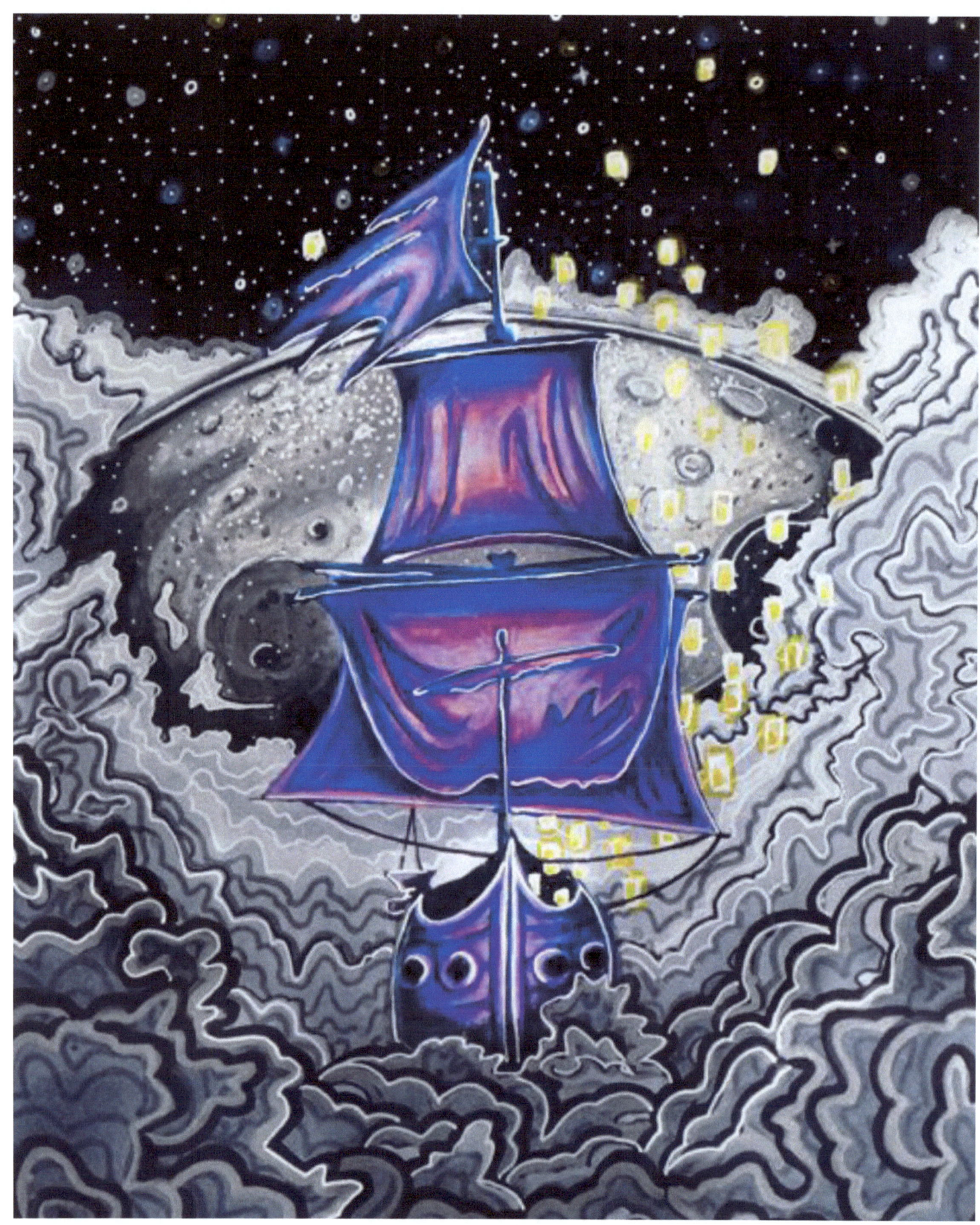

"Traveler of Worlds" Ink on Illustration Board. 8" x 12"

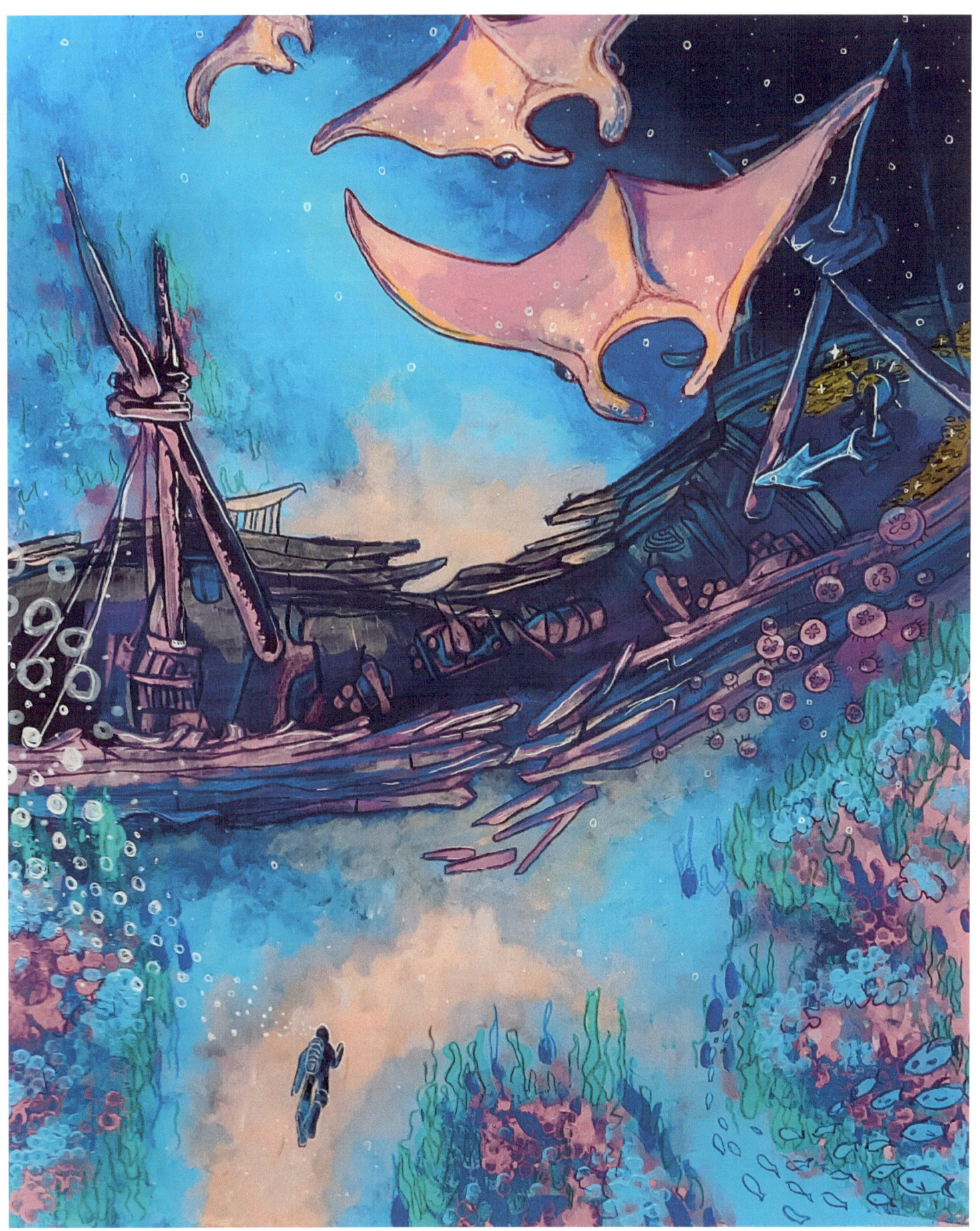

"Traveler of Worlds Continued" Acrylic on Illustration Board. 24" x 36"

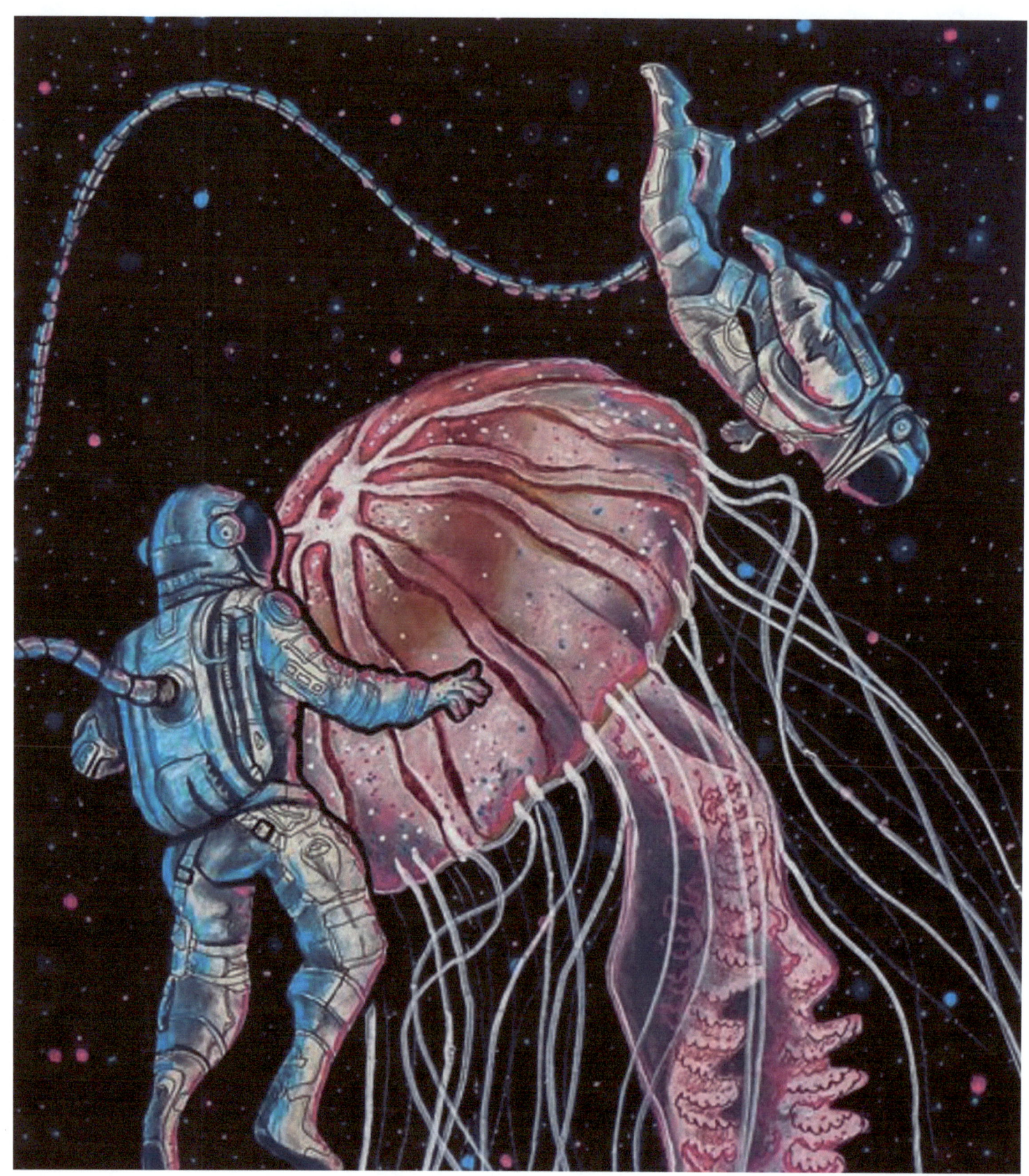

'Space Jellies" Acrylic on Illustration Board. 24" x 30"

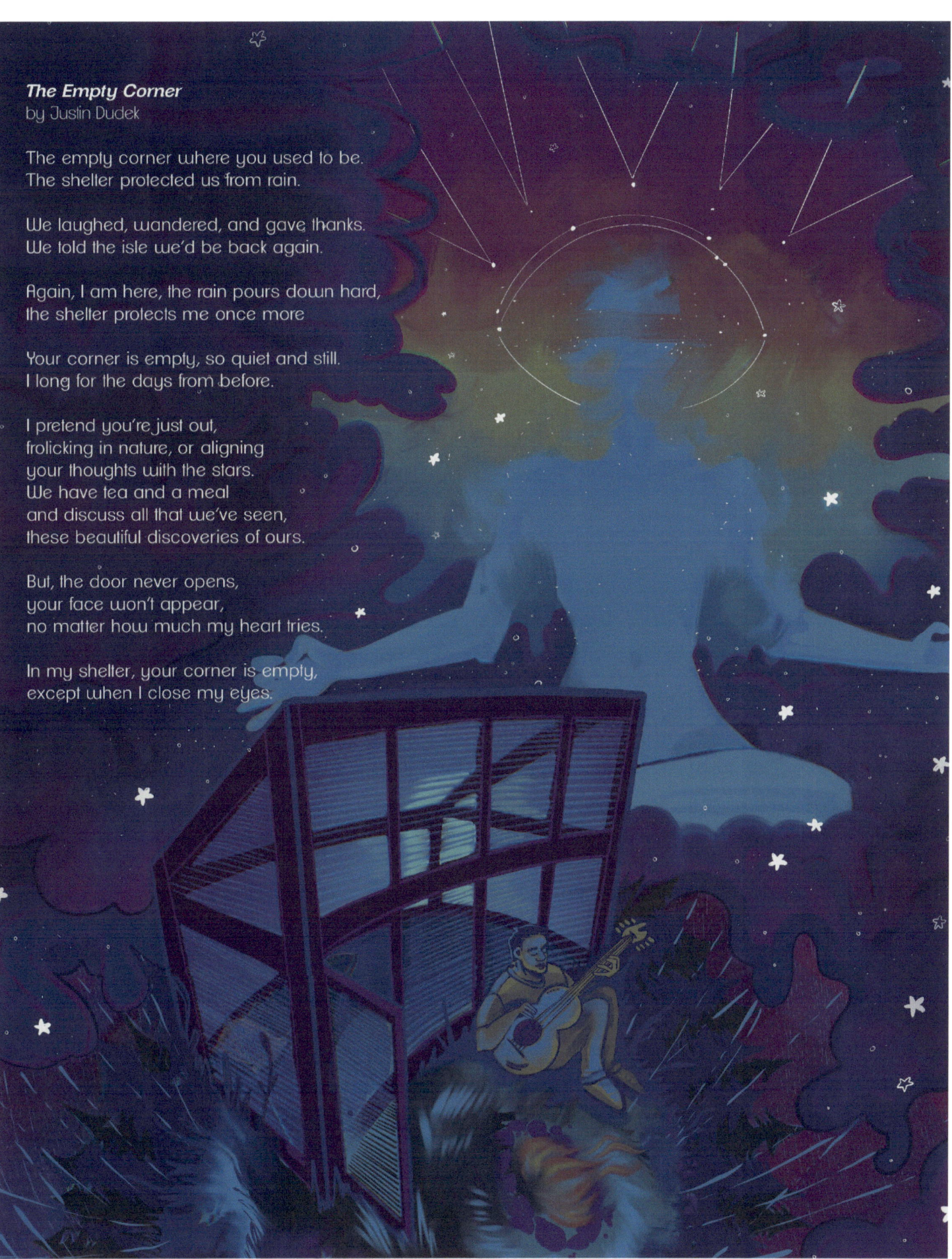

"The Empty Corner" Response Illustration. 8" x 11"

Thank You!

Happy to be with you,
My name is Ashlyn, I'm an Illustrator, Capricorn, and adventurer drawing dreamy, cosmic, and wavy works.

Originally from Las Vegas, Nevada, I have always lived in a different home every two years. My childhood consisted of beige, tuscan, desert welcoming the most beautiful passion for the galaxy and stars. As I traveled in my childhood, environments invited a passion for nautical life, and the sea.

I have had the wonderful pleasure of working with beautiful humans like: Mandi May with C. Edwards Press, Premier Family Dentistry, University of Wisconsin Milwaukee: Milk-Waukee, Faithbridge Church to name a few.

I sell my own collection of art prints in collaboration with INPRNT, where I drop a couple new prints every season! Check out my celestial jewelry line on artwithashlyn.com, and my Volunteer work at Lotus Legal Clinic.

@art.with.ashlyn   www.artwithashlyn.com   artwithashlyn.co@gmail.com

www.ingramcontent.com/pod-product-compliance
Lightning Source LLC
Chambersburg PA
CBHW040454220526
45473CB00004B/1633